Championship Volleyball Techniques and Drills

Championship

VOLLEYBALL

Techniques
and Drills

Sue Gozansky

PARKER PUBLISHING COMPANY
West Nyack, New York 10994

Library of Congress Cataloging-in-Publication Data

Gozansky, Sue.
    Championship volleyball techniques and drills.
    Includes index.
    ISBN 0-13-127639-5—ISBN 0-13-127621-2 (pbk)
      1.Volleyball—Coaching.   2. Volleyball—Training.
  I. Title.
  GV1015.5.C63G68   1983   83-4250
  796.32′5   CIP

Printed in the United States of America

20   19   18   17   16   15

ISBN 0-13-127639-5

ISBN 0-13-127621-2 (PBK)

ATTENTION: CORPORATIONS AND SCHOOLS

Parker books are available at quantity discounts with bulk purchase for educational, business, or sales promotional use. For information, please write to Prentice Hall Special Sales, 240 Frisch Court, Paramus, NJ 07652. Please supply: title of book, ISBN number, quantity, how the book will be used, date needed.

PARKER PUBLISHING COMPANY
West Nyack, New York 10994

On the World Wide Web at http://www.phdirect.com

To my mom, dad, and brother—
for their love and support.

Foreword

One of the most critical components of effective coaching is the teaching phase of individual skills. This book represents the best work in the English language on the processes necessary to develop high-level skills necessary to perform advanced tactics. So often in this country our coaches attempt to institute systems of play which their athletes lack the necessary technical skills to perform. Ms. Gozansky has done an outstanding job of logically and completely detailing the teaching progressions for each skill and the drills necessary to effect those teaching progressions. I think this book will serve to significantly improve the level of volleyball for both men and women in the United States. It is a major work that I am most pleased to recommend.

Douglas P. Beal, Ph.D.
USA Men's Volleyball Coach

Coaching Through Drills

Once enjoyed as a casual and recreational game, volleyball has developed into a powerful and complex athletic sport with techniques and tactics constantly being refined to higher levels. While the sport continues to grow on a worldwide level, there has been very little written to help teach the sport at the grassroots. This book helps fill the need for new and more detailed literature dealing with the specifics of volleyball and the complexities of coaching. As a practical handbook, basic techniques and styles of offensive and defensive play are examined, but the emphasis is primarily on drills designed to produce better-coached players. It is aimed at the beginning and intermediate level volleyball coach and the physical educator, but regardless of the amount of one's coaching or teaching experience, this manual can be used as a reference for new ideas to round out a repertory of coaching techniques. This book presents my approach to teaching techniques and gives examples of drills that I have personally designed and those I have acquired from coaches throughout the world.

The book covers each of the six basic volleyball skills—the pass, the serve, the set, the attack, the block, and floor defense. There are also chapters on team offense and team defense. A checklist is provided for each skill, and it is followed by drills to teach and practice that skill. The team offense and defense chapters explain various game strategies and deal more specifically with team offense, defense, and transition drills.

To best use this book, I recommend that you look at sequence figures while reviewing the technique checklists, and use the drill diagrams along with the verbal drill explanations. The letter symbols on the drill diagrams designate the correct court position. Diagrams of offensive and defensive positioning should be used along with the verbal tactical explanations.

Each drill in this book has one or more purposes designed to work on various aspects of the game. The purpose may include any of the following: 1) warm-up and conditioning, 2) movement training, 3) skills training, 4) tactic training, and 5) mental and physical toughness training.

Each drill in this book has a goal. The goal indicates what must be done to complete the drill. Drills that are competitive stress quality, and have as their goal a number of successful contacts before completion. Goals that stress quantity and repetition are practiced for a specific amount of time, with total concentration on learning or correcting a movement pattern, skill, or tactic. Intensity as well as physical conditioning is stressed in drills where players do many contacts in a short time span. Toughness drills emphasize both quality and quantity, as well as the intensity and stress of the competitive game.

Maxims that represent a coaching and teaching philosophy aimed toward perfection are included throughout the book. These maxims are important practice and game considerations for the player and the coach. These maxims not only relate to the accompanying drill but are appropriate in a multitude of situations.

I recommend that you do not simply copy these drills for use in your practice, but rather modify and personalize the drills to meet the needs of your team. This book gives you a solid base of drills on which to build. There are endless variations of these drills, and I hope that these drills will stimulate the creation of many new ones.

DRILL STYLES

Throughout the volleyball world two basic drill styles have developed—coach-oriented and player-oriented. Coach-oriented drills were popularized in Asia, whereas player-oriented drills were used in Eastern Europe. Both styles of drills have proven successful alone or in combination with the other. Each coach must decide which style best suits his or her situation.

Player-oriented drills are those in which a player works alone, with a partner, or in groups, while the coach, as an observer, moves from player to player to correct faults. The coach is able to view the entire situation and time is used effectively as all players participate at the same time.

In coach-oriented drills, the coach is directly involved in supervising and leading the drill, demanding that the skill be performed correctly and with maximum effort. Thus players are highly motivated to do their best for the coach and their peers. Players give encouragement to teammates and appreciate this team spirit when it is their turn to do the drill. Coach-oriented drills are helpful in working with beginners, where the skill level does not permit consistency in player-to-player drills. Coach-oriented drills require longer practice sessions to complete drills, and although an assistant coach is not vital, it is definitely helpful in reducing drill time. It is best to have a basket of about twenty-five balls for an average-sized team of fifteen players.

COACHING SKILLS

To teach and coach effectively, the coach must be able to demonstrate beginning to advanced techniques and movement patterns. The coach need not demonstrate skills in a competitive situation, but should be able to break the skill down for purposes of demonstration. To success-fully execute coach-oriented drills the coach must also have a repertoire of coaching skills.

Coaching Skill 1: Toss Precisely for Attacking

The coach must possess the ability to toss for the high or low attack. Tosses must be consistent in height and placement to help the players to learn attack techniques. A two-hand underhand toss with a long follow-through is most accurate. Practice tossing high and low sets while stand-ing about three feet from the net. Strive to toss ten consecutive and accurate high and low tosses.

Coaching Skill 2: Toss or Throw for Setting and Passing

The coach must be able to toss or bounce the ball so that the player can play the ball in the air or on the rebound (as the drill indicates) with a set or pass.

Coaching Skill 3: Attack Accurately for Defense

The coach must be able to simulate the hard, off-speed or tip attack from a standing position on the floor and from a tabletop attacking over the net. The coach should hit the ball directly to the player at a moderate speed until players learn proper technique. Then gradually as players become more advanced, speed and deception may be added to the at-tack. The coach must guarantee success by making certain that players are able to correctly play a high percentage of balls. To become proficient at this skill, practice hitting the ball against the wall as in handball. Stand about ten feet from the wall and hit the ball downward with a forearm and wrist snap action, causing the ball to hit close to your feet and rebound high on the wall. As the ball comes off the wall, reach up to the ball, and, using a spike action, hit the ball again to the floor. Strive for ten consecutive hits to the wall. Strive for accuracy first and as accuracy is achieved, the speed of the hit can be increased.

Coaching Skill 4: Serve for Accuracy

The coach must have the ability to serve to any spot on the court. The coach can guarantee success in serve reception by serving to players at moderate speed and progressing to more difficult serves as players become more proficient. Practice serving to targets on the court to increase accuracy. Both the overhand and sidearm serves are effective, but for continued serving the sidearm serve is less fatiguing.

Coaching Skill 5: Spiking Into the Block

From a standing position on a tabletop you must be able to hit a self-tossed ball across the net into, or off the blocker's hands. Good hand control on the attack is necessary to achieve this. Proper timing must be achieved between the blocker's jump and the coach's toss and hit.

In summary, to effectively utilize the coach-oriented drills you must have the ability to perform these coaching skills. It is as important for the coach to practice and perfect these coaching skills as it is for the players to perfect their game skills. The coach must also have the ability to recognize each player's mental and physical potential on a particular day and motivate and push each individual to his or her maximum performance. The coach can guarantee success to players by gradually increasing the difficulty of drills as each player improves. This gives players confidence and makes them "hungry" to exceed their reach.

Much success and happiness in your coaching.

Sue Gozansky

Acknowledgments

Special thanks to Moo Park, coach of the 1968 South Korean Women's Olympic Volleyball team, the 1976 Canadian Women's Olympic Volleyball team, and the 1971 United States Volleyball Association (USVBA) National Champion Los Angeles Renegades, to whom I owe much of my coaching philosophy, style, and success.

Special thanks are also due to all those coaches with whom I have worked at camps and clinics who have generously allowed me to observe their coaching techniques.

Lastly, thanks are due to Karoly Fogassy and his staff for their excellent artwork.

Table of Contents

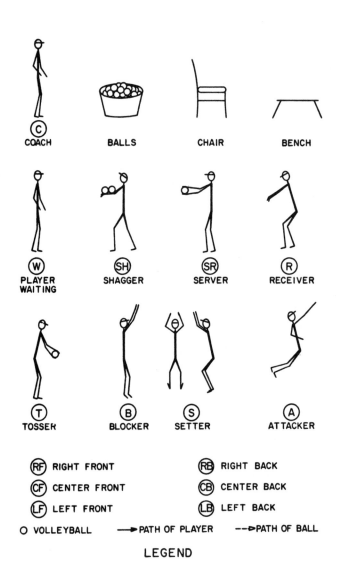

COACH   BALLS   CHAIR   BENCH

PLAYER WAITING   SHAGGER   SERVER   RECEIVER

TOSSER   BLOCKER   SETTER   ATTACKER

RF RIGHT FRONT   RB RIGHT BACK

CF CENTER FRONT   CB CENTER BACK

LF LEFT FRONT   LB LEFT BACK

O VOLLEYBALL   →PATH OF PLAYER   --▻PATH OF BALL

LEGEND

18

The Pass and Serve

THE PASS

The pass is the fundamental skill required for effective team play and must be mastered before any other skills can be successfully utilized in the game. The purpose of the pass is to direct the ball to the team's setter who initiates the offense. This pass is medium-high looping up about two to three feet above the net and descending near the setter at the net. There are two types of passes—the underhand and the overhand.

Underhand Pass

The underhand pass is used primarily to receive the serve. Serve reception is the key to your offense, and if a team cannot pass accurately it will pose no attack threat. A bad pass can result in losing a point, but even more critical, several bad passes can result in players' losing confidence and playing poorly.

The underhand pass is one of the easiest techniques in the game, requiring very little movement or strength. The most important factors are confidence and good footwork and positioning prior to the pass. It is a monotonous technique that is not as much fun to practice as other skills, but it is the most essential skill for proper execution of your offense.

Checklist

1. Ready position—a) feet shoulder distance apart, with one foot slightly ahead of the other; b) weight on the balls and the insides of feet with very little space between heels and floor; c) knees bent and turned in slightly; d) trunk bent forward, knees ahead of toes, shoulders ahead of knees; e) arms extended out from body, hands apart and down by knees.
2. Quickly determine where the ball will go and move body behind and under the path of the ball, body facing direction of the intended pass, hips open to oncoming ball.
3. Stop, assume a balanced position and step to the target. When passing to the right, step with the right foot. When passing to the left, step with the left foot.
4. Trunk slightly tilted forward.

5. Arms brought together straight in front of body to form a solid platform. The arms never bend in the entire execution of the pass.
6. Heel of hands and thumbs firmly held together (felt in shoulders). Fingers interlaced to first knuckle or hands held in interlocked position (Figure 1-1).

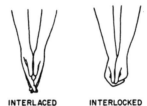

Figure 1-1   INTERLACED   INTERLOCKED

7. Hands and wrists turned down allowing elbow extension and straight arms.
8. Play ball at the body midline whenever possible, contacting the ball out from the body at about knee level (Figure 1-2).

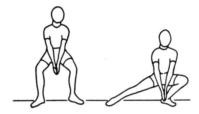

Figure 1-2

9. When it is not possible to play the ball at the midline, open the hips, turn the shoulders down to face the target, and take the ball out to the side (Figure 1-3).

Figure 1-3

10. Pass the ball on the wide fleshy surface of the forearms, two to three inches above the wrist.
11. Watch the ball with the eyes as it contacts the arms. Do not jerk the head down.
12. Shoulders and arms face the setter and contribute the main force in the pass. Extend the shoulders and arms forward and slightly up-

ward with a controlled arm swing. Swing is directed from shoulders, with movement observed in the shoulder joint and absent in the elbow joint (Figure 1-4).

1.   2.   3.   4.   5.   **Figure 1-4**

13. Guide the ball to the setter. Follow through in the direction of the desired ball flight.
14. The angle of the forearms determines the direction in which the ball will rebound.
15. At the completion of the pass the knees remain bent, body weight is forward toward the setter, arms are straight and about shoulder height.

Overhand Pass (Figure 1-5)

Either the underhand or overhand pass may be used to pass the free ball (a ball that is not attacked by the opponents but is passed over the net softly). The overhand pass is the preferred pass for the free ball because this technique provides a longer contact period and allows for better accuracy and control. Since the overhand pass must be played above the forehead, the underhand pass must be used when the ball is too low.

1   2   3   4   **Figure 1-5**

Checklist

1. Ready position—a) feet shoulder distance apart, with one foot slightly ahead of the other; b) weight on the balls and insides of feet

with very little space between heels and floor; c) knees bent and turned in slightly; d) trunk bent forward; e) hands held comfortably at chest level.

2. Move quickly behind and under the ball with body facing the direction of intended pass (square off to target).
3. Stop, feet shoulder distance apart and staggered slightly, preferably with the right foot forward. Knees bent ready to push into the set.
4. Head tilted back, looking up to ball.
5. Hands move up, elbows shoulder high, forearms parallel to the floor (prior to contact, hands never above head).
6. Fingers spread wide apart, slightly tensed, and shaped to the form of a volleyball.
7. Wrists tilted back, thumbs down, the thumb and index finger form a triangle. The triangle determines the angle of the elbows.
8. Set begins with simultaneous extension of legs and arms forward and upward into the ball.
9. Fingers equally and simultaneously "grab" ball.
10. Fingers relaxed, allowing the ball to contact the fleshy pads of all the fingers, but not the palms. The thumb and first three fingers of each hand are the main contact points. The little finger serves to guide and stabilize the ball.
11. Wrists flick forward into ball. Receiving the ball is like a compressed spring and releasing the ball is the extension of the spring.
12. Arms and hands extend up quickly to contact the ball above and in front of the forehead.
13. On follow-through entire body is extended in direction of set, palms forward, fingers extended. Aim for a lengthy hand contact for best control and accuracy. A soft touch is achieved by the entire body accelerating into the ball with an equal push of the arms and legs.
14. To check position, throw the ball into the air, and with the proper body, arm, and hand position allow the ball to drop into the properly cupped fingers without rebounding. Check finger, thumb, and body position.

MAXIM: *Use drill progressions to guarantee success and proper learning of skills:*

A. 1. Model skill without the ball, slow to quick (movement without the ball).
   2. Perform skill with the ball, limiting movement (static).
   3. Perform skill with faster ball speed and greater distances (dynamic).
   4. Stress accuracy (targets).

5. Stress successful contacts (goals).
6. Stress mental considerations (tactics).
7. Stress pre- and post-skill movement (linking actions).
8. Stress results under any circumstances (toughness).
B. 1. Simple one-skill drills with static, then dynamic, movement.
2. Simple combination drills with a combination of skills; each individual repeatedly performing one skill at a time.
3. Complex combination drills involving one individual performing a sequence of skills.
4. Complex combination drills with group or team performing a sequence of drills.

PARTNER DRILLS

Partner at net tosses, backcourt player performs skill. When skill level warrants, both players perform drill alternately.

Pass Over Line

Purpose: Technique and accuracy training.

Goal: Specific time period or one set of 30. If ball drops, drill starts at zero.

Description: Partners about ten feet apart, pass overhand or underhand over a line, beside the net or near a wall. Repeat with the overhand pass. Pass about ten to twelve feet high.

MAXIM: *For each skill and drill there is always a higher level. Movement to each level must be earned and a practical degree of proficiency and success must be reached.*

Pass Long-Short

Purpose: Technique and movement training.

Goal: Specific time period or one set of 30. If ball drops, drill starts at zero.

Description: Partners about ten feet apart, overhand or underhand pass alternating long and short passes so there is continual forward and backward movement. Pass about ten to twelve feet high. Stress passing from a balanced stationary position.

MAXIM: *Establish clear practice goals. The more meaningful the practice is perceived as being, the greater the desire to work hard.*

Pass Side to Side

Purpose: Technique and movement training.

Goal: Specific time period or one set of 30. If ball drops, drill starts at zero.

Description: Partners about ten feet apart alternating overhand or underhand passes to the right and left of partner to insure side stepping to the ball. Pass about ten to twelve feet high. Stress playing the ball directly in front of the body, shoulders and arms facing target.

Pass In/Out, Out/In

Purpose: Technique and movement training.

Goal: Specific time period or one set of 30. If ball drops, drill starts at zero.

Description: Partners about ten feet apart executing overhand or underhand pass with movement before and after pass. For in/out, move three small steps forward after set, backpedal three steps, stop and pass. For out/in, move three small steps backward after pass, move forward three steps, stop and pass.

Straddle-Sit Pass

Purpose: Active rest (practicing volleyball skills that allow cardiovascular rest and recovery), and to stress proper hand, arm, and shoulder position.

Goal: Specific time period.

Description: Partners seated in straddle position, three feet apart, facing each other. Overhead pass slightly to the right or left of body midline forcing partner to lean so as to position the upper body behind the ball.

Pass and Sit-Ups

Purpose: Overhand pass technique.

Goal: 25 passes and sit-ups each.

Description: Partners seated in straddle position three feet apart, facing each other, lie back, sit up, and receive pass from partner. Continuous pass and sit-up.

Chest-Position Pass

Purpose: Overhand pass technique and active rest.

Goal: 15 passes each.

Description: Partners facing each other lying on chest about three feet apart, both pass ball overhand. Must arch up to pass ball.

Sit-Up and Backset

Purpose: Backset technique, active rest.

Goal: Ten backsets, change tasks.

Description: One partner lying on back, other player in standing position directly behind partner's head. Standing player tosses ball over head of partner. Player on floor sits up and backsets ball back to partner.

MAXIM: *Movement must be included in all drills as quickly as possible. Rarely in the game does the ball come directly to you.*

Over the Net Pass—Shuttle Drill (Figure 1-6)

Purpose: Overhand and underhand pass technique training.

Team Goal: Group completes ten to 100 good underhand passes. If ball drops or error is made drill begins over at zero. Repeat with the overhand pass.

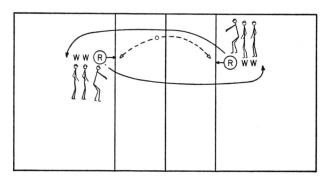

Figure 1-6

Description: Two groups of five to eight players on each court pass the ball about twelve feet high and over the net to a position near the ten-foot line. Players pass and move to the right and to the end of the opposite line. Continuous passing across the net. Stress quick movement to the ball and passing from a stationary position. As skill level increases, add the jump set.

MAXIM: *High number of repetitions without a miss develops good concentration.*

MAXIM: *Care must be taken to set realistic goals suited to players' abilities. Goals must be difficult but attainable.*

Pass to Target With Tosser (Figure 1-7)

Purpose: Overhand and underhand pass technique and accuracy training.

Team Goal: 25 good overhand passes and 25 good underhand passes.

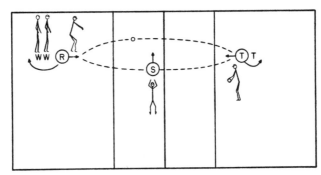

Figure 1-7

Description: Two groups of approximately six players on each court. Groups divided into receivers, setters, and tossers. The tosser tosses ball with a two-hand underhand toss to back row receiver and moves to the end of the tossing line. Receiver passes to setter. Setter catches the ball and rolls it under the net back to the tosser. Group changes tasks after 25 good passes. To keep the drill moving rapidly the tosser and the setter each start with one ball. As one ball leaves the tosser's hand the setter rolls the other ball back to the tosser so the receivers are able to pass one ball after another in rapid succession. Stress court talk—the receiver calls "mine" before the pass is made.

MAXIM: *Players must respond to each drill without being careless. Do not allow players to practice improper technique. Do not let an error go uncorrected.*

Pass to Target with Coach Tossing (Figure 1-8)

Purpose: Overhand and underhand pass technique and accuracy training.

Team Goal: 100 good passes to set target (coach designates overhand or underhand).

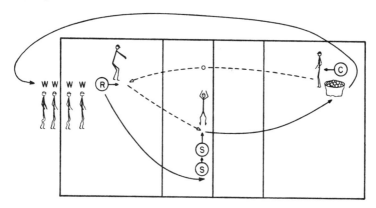

Figure 1-8

Description: Similar to pass to target with tosser drill. The coach takes the place of the tosser, thus regulating where the toss will go. The coach can keep the drill moving at a rapid pace and challenge the players with more difficult tosses or with a serve. One receiving line, one setter, and one on-deck setter. The coach tosses or serves the ball to the receiver. The receiver passes the ball to the set target. The setter catches the pass, runs under the net, hands the ball back to the coach, and then circles back to the end of the receiving line. The on-deck setter moves to the setter's position and the receiver is on deck. It is important for the coach to vary the tossing position, speed, and direction of the toss. Repeat drill with receiving line in left and right back positions on the court.

MAXIM: *Require and demand success. Drills must contain specific goals that must be attained to complete the drill.*

Touch Net—Backpedal—Serve Reception (Figure 1-9)

Purpose: Serve reception training.

Team Goal: 50 good passes to set target.

Description: Two receiving lines and one setter. Two receivers begin drill facing the net and holding net with both hands. Additional players wait in line just off the court and to the side. When the coach slaps the ball, the two receivers backpedal quickly and prepare to pass a deep serve. One receiver calls "mine" and passes to the set target, then takes the place of the setter. The setter catches and returns the ball to the coach. Both players then go to the end of their receiving line. The next two receivers immediately move to their position at the net as the previous receivers

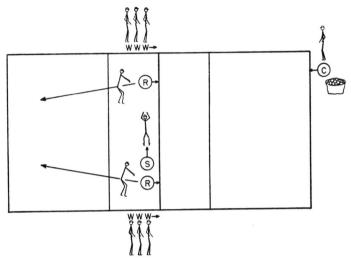

Figure 1-9

backpedal. Repeat drill with receivers beginning on the endline, and moving forward to receive a short serve. *Advanced variation*: Coach serves while standing on a table top. This makes the serve come harder and at a more downward trajectory.

MAXIM: Communicate with your teammates. Call "mine."

MAXIM: Good footwork prior to the pass is foremost. Many errors are caused by bad footwork. Move quickly to the ball. Pass from a stationary position.

THE SERVE

Technically, it is the purpose of the serve to initiate play, but it is also a means of attack. Only by serving can you score points, so it is important to keep the ball in play while at the same time serving aggressively in an attempt to score a direct point or to force the opponents into a disadvantaged position.

Underhand Serve

When a skill level warrants, it is recommended that the overhand or sidearm serve be taught. However, consideration should be given to the use of the underhand serve as a progression to higher levels of technique. Players, especially very young ones, generally have greater control of the underhand serve. This control eliminates many unnecessary service errors and creates a more continuous and exciting game. Placement is also more effective and allows players to begin using tactics at an early stage. Finally, reception is more effective with the slower trajectory of the underhand serve. It allows use of all game skills without the serve's dominating the game. When the ability level of players has increased to a sufficient degree, the overhand or sidearm serve should be used.

Underhand Serve Checklist (Figure 1-10)

1. Stand facing net.
2. Leg opposite hitting arm slightly forward, weight on front foot.
3. Non-hitting hand holds ball in the palm of hand at waist level.
4. Hitting arm down by side ready for backswing.
5. Toss ball up and forward to above chest level.
6. Bring hitting arm back behind body with elbow slightly bent.
7. Body weight transferred forward as arm moves forward to contact ball.
8. Hand cupped or in fist on contact.
9. Contact ball at about waist level in front of body.
10. Contact lower portion of ball slightly behind and under ball.
11. Quick contact with a short follow-through.
12. Hand and foot pointing in direction of intended flight.

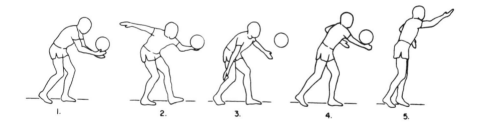

Figure 1-10

Floater Serve

The floater serve is the most common advanced type of serve in today's game. This serve is similar to the knuckleball in baseball. It floats through the air and may move from side to side or suddenly drop to the floor. It is difficult to receive because the flight of the ball is unpredictable. The floater serve may be performed while facing the net (overhand), or from a side to the net position (sidearm). The sidearm floater is advantageous for young players and those with less shoulder strength than is required for the overhand serve. The sidearm serve allows for greater arm

motion prior to contact, enabling even a small player to serve aggressively. The effectiveness of the serves depends solely on the execution—not
on the style chosen.

Overhand Floater Checklist (Figure 1-11)

1. Stand facing the net, feet slightly staggered, foot opposite from
   serving arm slightly forward and pointed to the target, weight on
   back foot.
2. Ball held with both hands, holding hand underneath ball, hitting
   hand on top.
3. Arms held out in front of body parallel to floor.
4. Just prior to toss, step forward with the front foot in the direction of
   the target, transferring the body weight forward.
5. Ball is tossed upward over head about two feet high and in front of
   serving shoulder. Hitting arm is drawn back behind the ear with
   elbow at shoulder level (simulating a throwing action). Tossing arm
   remains up.

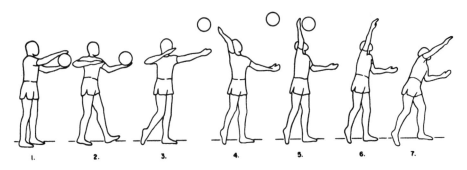

Figure 1-11

6. Shoulders drawn back to allow for body rotation into ball.
7. When ball begins to drop, shoulder and arm rotates into hit, with
   body weight transferred forward.
8. Contact is made in front of the body and above the head with the
   arm almost straight.
9. Contact is made on the palm of the open hand with wrist remaining
   firm. Hand and forearm act as a unit.
10. Contact center back of ball with quick action and very little follow-
    through.
11. Palm facing target at completion of serve.
12. Strive for low trajectory over net.

Sidearm Floater Checklist (Figure 1-12)

1. Stand sideways to the net.
2. Feet shoulder distance apart, knees slightly bent.
3. Ball arm up, extended out from body forward and toward net, hitting arm relaxed, held straight or slightly bent at chest level.
4. Toss ball upward one to two feet above head, slightly in front of the forward foot, and parallel to the net. (Short step with foot opposite hitting arm may be taken just prior to toss.)
5. As the ball is tossed, the body leans backwards as both legs bend and the hips rotate back; the hitting arm swings back with arm straight and hand near hip.
6. Movement for the hit begins with sharp rotation of the hips, and shoulder extending forward and upward.
7. Legs extend up and weight is transferred forward.
8. Hitting arm swings upward in a windmill motion.
9. Shoulder of hitting hand leads arm; forearm and hand stay slightly back.

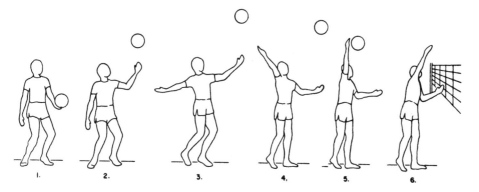

Figure 1-12

10. The tossing arm moves down and weight is shifted to forward foot.
11. At contact, body is opened to the front with hips and shoulders facing net.
12. Ball is hit at highest point above the forward shoulder with arm almost straight.
13. Contact with ball on palm of open hand with wrist remaining firm.
14. At moment of contact, palm faces direction of target.
15. Contact center back of ball with quick action and very little follow-through.

Topspin Serve (Figure 1-13)

The topspin serve is an advanced type of serve that is hit with a great deal of speed and forward spin causing it to drop rapidly to the floor. The trajectory of the ball is easily determined, but its rapid movement makes it difficult to pass.

The body position for the topspin serve is similar to that for the overhead floater, but it is the position and method of contact that creates the topspin.

The hand is open and makes contact on the lower section of the ball. The hand and wrist snaps vigorously over the ball and the arm follows through away from the body. The ball is hit upward and forward with a strong, quick wrist and forearm snap. This action causes the ball to spin.

Figure 1-13

MAXIM: *Most important condition to avoid errors: Attentively look at the ball in all stages of executing the serve.*

DRILLS

Throw and Serve 2s

Purpose: Beginner serve training, technique and strength.

Goal: Specific time period.

Description: Partners midcourt from each other and on opposite sides of the net. Holding ball with one hand above head, player executes a one-handed throw over the net to partner. Player releases ball with arm extended, elbow above the shoulder. After several successful tosses by each player, they serve over the net to one another. Players back up several steps and repeat the above sequence. This process is continued until players are serving from endline to endline. Stress serve contact out in front of the body. Practice the service toss and let the ball bounce to visually check that the ball is in front of the body and in line with the hitting shoulder.

MAXIM: *Keep the serving action simple: Minimum action for maximum results.*

Serve to Wall Contest

Purpose: Beginner serve training.

Goal: First team to 15 wins.

Description: Two teams stand in a separate line behind a line about 25 to 30 feet from a wall. One player assumes a serving position behind the line and the second player in line stands halfway between the server and the wall, ready to catch the serve on the rebound. The server then serves the ball to the wall above the tape mark (seven to ten feet high). If the serve is above the tape and is caught by the receiver a point is scored. Server becomes catcher and catcher moves to the end of the line. The first team to 15 wins.

MAXIM: *You win or lose with points. The game is not over until the final point. Use game-related numbers, for example, 15 points to complete the drill, or 16, 17, or 18.*

Serve and Catch

Purpose: Serve training.

Goal: Specific time period.

Description: Players divided equally on each side of the court. One ball for every two players. Players with a ball serve from the proper service area. Other players attempt to receive the ball by catching. Each time you have possession of the ball you serve.

MAXIM: *Practice the serve, both when players are fresh and when they are fatigued, as occurs in the game.*

MAXIM: *Always direct the serve to a specific target. Always attempt to make serves both accurate and tough.*

Easy, Medium, Hard Serves

Purpose: Serve training.

Goal: Specific time period.

Description: Players positioned along endline on both sides of the court. Players serve first ball fairly easy; second ball served at medium strength; third ball served hard, but all balls are expected to go "in." Repeat sequence. Players should know their own ability and be knowledgeable of what they can and cannot do with their serves. *Variation:* Players attempt their toughest serves without worrying about errors. After a specific time period players attempt to serve their toughest serve that they feel will be "in." There are times in the game that it is very important not to lose the serve. Stress the importance of tough and controlled serves.

MAXIM: *Allow players time in practice to work on tough serves without penalty.*

MAXIM: *The better the opposition receiver and setter, the better the serve must be to effectively eliminate the good attack.*

Serve to Target and Jog (Figure 1-14)

Purpose: Serve accuracy training.

Individual Goal: Nine out of ten serves to each target.

Team Goal: Point scored for each served ball that hits the target. A point is subtracted for each serving error (ball hit out or into the net). The score may not go below zero. 15 points to complete the drill.

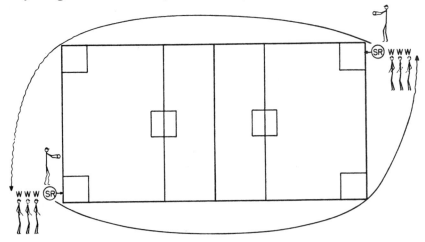

Figure 1-14

Description: The first player in each serving line serves to a specific target area. After the serve, jog and shag the ball and return to the end of the opposite serving line. Serve to target *A* until the goal is reached, then to target *B*, and so on. Jogging adds the element of conditioning to the serving drill.

MAXIM: *The serve is an offensive weapon. Keep the pressure on the opponent; serve aggressively and with control.*

MAXIM: *Just before you serve, look confidently across the net and determine your serve strategy.*

Target Serves

Purpose: Serve to target.

Description: Players serving from service area.

Goal/Competitions:

1. Serve 15 deep crosscourt serves and 15 deep line serves. The winner is the first to score 30 serves to the targets.
2. Serve between chairs, as you would want to serve between opponents.
3. Serve to targets for prizes.
4. Best record of number to target in a row.
5. Best record of consecutive good serves.
6. Best record of number to target out of ten with fewest service errors.
7. Best record of serves to targets in specific time period.
8. Look to coach for hand signal indicating the position of the court to direct serve.
9. Serve 15 to one specific target, serving at least five in a row before moving to the next target.
10. Serve to target after intense exercise. Create physical fitness conditions close to actual game situations.

MAXIM: *Discipline and concentration: No talking during serve practice.*

30 Seconds—No-Miss Serves

Purpose: Serving consistency and mental toughness.

Team Goal: No serving errors for 30 seconds.

Description: Players divided equally on each side of the court and positioned behind the endline. On signal from coach the time begins and all players prepare to serve. If one player commits a serving error the time starts over. Repeat the drill no more than three times. If all serves are "in" within the first 30 seconds, and the drill is completed, congratulate the team. Stress the importance of complete concentration on the serve. If there is not sufficient room for all players to be serving from the proper service area, it is important that those players positioned on the left side of the court serve straight across.

MAXIM: *Practice must prepare athletes psychologically for the competitive task of the game.*

MAXIM: *There are certain times when it is more important to serve "in" than to risk a difficult serve.*

No-Miss Serve Situation

Purpose: Serving consistency and mental toughness.

Individual Goal: Serve "in."

Description: Players are divided equally on each side of the court. One or two players serve simultaneously from the service area. The coach sets up a game situation, for instance, "The score is 13 to 14 and we need a tough serve down the line." Players who err must do 15 push-ups. This drill is most easily performed within other serving drills, but can be used at any time during the practice.

MAXIM: *Worst serving error is serving into the net. Give the opponent an opportunity to err.*

MAXIM: *Discipline and concentration: Assign penalties for service errors in "no-miss" situations.*

Serve to Target Series

Purpose: Serving consistency, control, and accuracy.

Goal: Specific time period.

Description: Players are divided equally on each side of the court. One or two players may serve simultaneously from the right side of the court. 1) Players serve first to the deep down-the-line target. When they successfully hit that target they serve to the deep crosscourt target, and then to the short middle target. Players aim for a new target after they successfully hit the previous one. Each player serves one ball and moves to the end of his/her own line. 2) Serve ten balls to each target. Of the ten, count the good serves to the target.

MAXIM: *First priority in serving is accuracy. The second priority is speed.*

MAXIM: *Discipline and concentration: First serve in each practice serve drill must be in (penalty situation).*

MAXIM: *Challenge players by decreasing target area size as servers become more accurate.*

Serve Around the World (Figure 1-15)

Purpose: Serving consistency, control, accuracy.

Individual Goal: Serve "around the world" by serving to each of the six zones on the court.

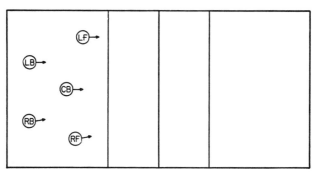

Figure 1-15

Description: Targets are placed on the court in the opponent's service reception positions. Players serve from the right side of the court and aim between the targets, starting from the area around zone one and progressing to zone six. (See zones in Figure 7-8.) Player starts by serving to zone one, and if successful, serves to zone two, and so on. If an error is made, server begins over at zone one.

MAXIM: *Never serve directly to a player; serve in the seams between players.*

Timed Serve Reception

Purpose: Serve and serve reception training.

Goal: Best record of successful passes to the target in specific time period.

Description: One right and one left back receiver, one setter, and one or more servers. Server serves and receiver passes to setter, who catches ball and rolls back to servers. Servers serve immediately after setter catches pass. *Variations:* 1) Place a sheet across net to shield ball until last possible moment. 2) Three players receiving in a triangle position— that is, right, left, and center back positions—two minutes, then rotate positions.

MAXIM: *Forget the bad pass. Concentrate on the next one and correct a previous error.*

Serve and Reception Shuttle (Figure 1-16)

Purpose: Serve and serve reception training.

Team Goal: 25 passes to the target from the right back position and 25 passes from the left back position.

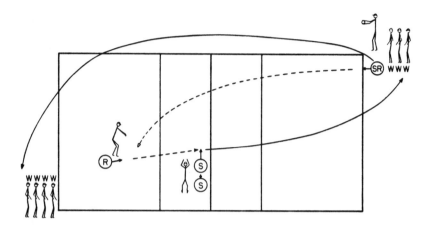

Figure 1-16

Description: One line of receivers, one setter, one on-deck setter, and a serving line. The first receiver moves into the right back receiving position and passes the served ball to the setter. The setter catches the pass and moves to the end of the serving line. The receiver becomes the on-deck setter and a new receiver moves into position. The server moves to the end of the receiving line. After 25 good passes to the target, the drill is repeated from the left-back receiving position. To keep drill moving rapidly, servers serve next ball immediately after the setter catches the ball. *Variations:* 1) Setters set ball high forward or back and must run to catch ball before it bounces. 2) Add two backcourt receivers at left and right back positions. Team passes 50 times to the target to complete drill. With two receivers the individual drill is now a team drill and receivers must determine who will pass the ball.

MAXIM: *The pass should be practiced as quickly as possible in combination with other skills.*

Serve Reception—3's (Figure 1-17)

Purpose: Serve and reception training and consistency.

Description: Two groups of three on each court, one server, one receiver, one setter. Receiver may select any reception position desired. Servers

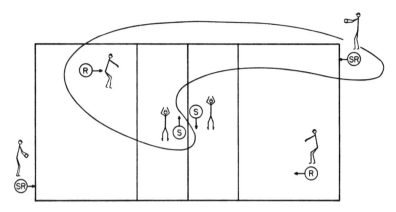

Figure 1-17

serve from proper service area at right. Setter acts as target, counter, and shagger.

Goal:

1. Specific number of good passes, then rotate.
2. Specific number of consecutive good passes to rotate.
3. Around the world. Pass to the target from each service reception position.
4. Three in a row. The server or receiver must score three consecutive points to win. The receiver must pass the ball accurately to the setter to score (setter counts for server and receiver). If the server errs or does not serve within the receiver's area of responsibility, the receiver scores a point. If the receiver errs, the server scores a point. Three consecutive points and the winner changes positions with the setter. Loser remains in same position.

MAXIM: *A key element to winning is the ability to earn consecutive points. Strive for consistent positive plays.*

Serve Reception—4's (Figure 1-18)

Purpose: Serve and serve reception training and teamwork.

Goal: Ten good passes.

Description: Two groups of four on each court. Each group has two receivers, one setter, and one server. Receivers assume either adjacent back-row positions (right and left back) or staggered front- and backcourt positions (right back, right front). Receiver takes serve and passes to set target. After each good pass receivers switch positions. Receiver completes ten good passes and takes position of server or setter.

Figure 1-18

MAXIM: Use visual and verbal communication on serve reception for better passing. Receiver calls "mine," nonreceivers call "in" or "out" on balls close to the line, and open up to and face the passer.

Serve Reception—4's (Figure 1-18)

Purpose: Serve and serve reception training.

Goal: Greatest number of good passes wins.

Description: Two groups of four on each court. Each group has two receivers, one setter, and one server. Receivers assume either adjacent back row positions or staggered front- and backcourt positions. Server from each group serves 20 balls (ten to each receiver). Receivers earn one point for an accurate pass to the setter (setter counts). After 20 serves players rotate positions. Individual in each group with best number of successful passes wins.

MAXIM: Early communication helps teamwork. Strive to call "mine" before the ball crosses the net.

Triangle Serve Reception (Figure 1-19)

Purpose: Serve reception training and teamwork.

Team Goal: Setter receives 15 good passes.

Description: Two groups on each court performing drill at same time. Each group divided into three receivers, two servers, and one setter. Receivers positioned in a triangle with two deep backcourt players and one receiver at the top of the triangle. Receiver passes serve to setter who catches ball and rolls it back to the servers on the same side of the court.

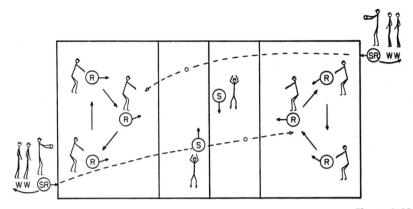

Figure 1-19

The setter counts five good passes and the receivers rotate positions within the triangle. After 15 good passes, the players change tasks. The center front player must determine quickly whether or not to pass the ball, and must "open up" and face the receiver who will pass. *Variation:* The team's setters play the set position, and set every pass. Setters mentally check each set and make adjustments on the next set.

MAXIM: *If you are not receiving the serve, you must plan for the bad pass and be ready to help out.*

Servers vs. Receivers (Figure 1-20)

Purpose: Serve and serve reception training.

Team Goal: Receiver pass ten to target.

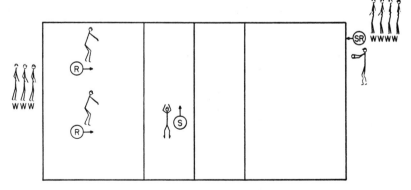

Figure 1-20

Description: Two groups—servers and receivers. Two receivers positioned in right and left back. One setter (from the receiving group) positioned at the net as the set target. One server at a time serves to the receivers. Alternate serves to right and left back receivers. After each pass a new receiver moves onto the court. Servers serve immediately after the setter catches the ball. After ten good passes (or ten service errors—one point is scored by the receivers for a service error) the groups run to opposite side of the net and change tasks. *Variation:* Three receivers in a triangle position.

MAXIM: *The game starts at 10-10. It is critical to the outcome of the game to not lose the serve at this time.*

MAXIM: *Determine where the ball will go by "reading" the server's position and contact point on the ball.*

The Set

The purpose of the set is to place the ball in a position in which your offense can attack the ball. A setter's first priority is accuracy in height and placement to help the hitter to be consistent. A second priority is combining this accuracy with the ability to make the proper decision regarding whom to set, the type of set, and to do so quickly and deceptively.

Although the team setter has the main responsibility to captain the offense, all players must be able to set the ball high to the outside attacker. The basic overhand set is a high set, about ten feet above the net and one to two feet from the net landing near the sideline. This set may be directed forward or back (backset). There are many variations of sets that can be utilized in the game. These sets vary in both height and position along the net. These set variations will be discussed in the chapter on team offense.

FRONT SET (Figure 2-1)

The basics of setting are similar to those for the overhand pass technique, demonstrated in Chapter 1, with these exceptions:

1. The team setter must maintain a more up and down, balanced posture prior to the set. This disguises the set direction until the last moment.
2. A greater knee bend and follow-through is used for high and distant sets.

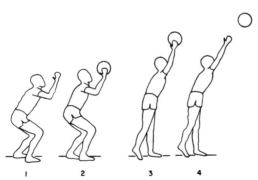

1   2   3   4

Figure 2-1

3. Good footwork is needed to reach distant passes. Run to the ball, stop, pivot to face the target, and set. Plant feet to assume a good basic body position, bend knees, and set.

BACKSET (Figure 2-2)

To execute the backset, the hips move forward upon contact with the ball, the back is arched, and the weight is transferred to the forward foot. The entire body follows through in the direction of the set with the head following the flight of the ball.

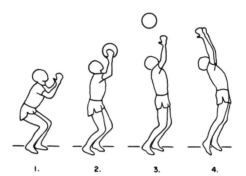

Figure 2-2   1.   2.   3.   4.

UNDERHAND SET (Figure 2-3)

When the ball is not sufficiently high to set the ball overhand, the underhand set is utilized. This technique is similar to the underhand pass demonstrated in Chapter 1, with the exception that the ball is contacted out to the side of the body. One shoulder is lowered to allow the arms to be behind and under the ball facing the target. With a controlled arm swing and body pivot the ball is directed to the target. Lift up on the ball and raise the knees slightly to gain additional height.

Figure 2-3   1.   2.   3.

JUMP SET (Figure 2-4)

The jump set is utilized:

1. For balls passed close to the net
2. For balls going over the net and
3. For quickness in getting the ball to the attacker

The set is executed primarily with the wrists and a quick extension of the arms. Run to the ball, hop and jump, squaring off in the air to face the intended direction of the set. The setter must jump and contact the ball at the top of the jump.

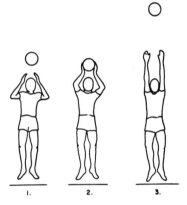

Figure 2-4

SET WITH ROLL (Figure 2-5)

To set a ball that is low and to the side, move quickly to where the ball is dropping. The last step before reaching the ball is a long one. The body weight is transferred onto one leg, and the body continues to move under the ball, the shoulders turning to face the target direction. The set is executed with a quick extension of the arms. The center of gravity is carried past the base of support and this momentum follows through with a full or half roll (Figure 2-5). For a low set in front of you, set and roll backwards (Figure 2-6).

Figure 2-5

I. 2. 3. 4. 5.

Figure 2-6

DRILLS

Catch and Throw—2's

Purpose: Set technique training.

Goal: Specific time period.

Description: Partner holds ball out in front of you; you place both hands on the ball making a triangle of the thumb and first fingers of each hand. Raise your hands with the ball to a position just above the forehead; upper arms parallel to floor, feet in a staggered position with the right foot forward, knees bent. From this position toss the ball straight up into the air by extending the arms quickly upward Catch the ball in the original starting position, that is, a balanced position with the right foot forward, knees bent, and hands just above the forehead. Continue to catch and throw while partner checks your position. Then change tasks.

MAXIM: *The follow-through results show what happened previously in the skill. Check and correct hand and body positioning.*

Freeze, Check, and Correct—2's

Purpose: Set technique training. Freeze, check, and correct hand and body positioning.

Goal: Specific time period.

Description: Partners stand about 15 feet apart and catch and throw ball back and forth using proper setting techniques. Partners freeze their position after each catch and after each throw in order to check, and if necessary correct, their position. Check points on the catch: balanced position, feet staggered, right foot forward, upper arms parallel to the floor, all ten fingers on the ball, ball not touching the palm of the hand, and ball in front of body at forehead level. Check points on the throw: balanced position, weight on the forward foot, arms and legs extended fully in the direction of the toss. Players go slowly at first, freezing, checking, and correcting each catch and throw. As player technique improves, movement is added and throw gradually develops into partners' setting back and forth without freezing the ball.

Individual Ball Handling Drills

Purpose: Underhand pass, overhand pass, and set technique development through constant repetition.

Individual Goal: Three sets of 15 or one set of 50. If ball is dropped or error is made, drill starts over at zero. If skill level varies significantly, set individual goals for each player.

Description: Players are positioned comfortably around gym, each with a ball. Coach designates specific drill to be performed. All sets must be a minimum of 12 feet high.

1. Teach use of hands and wrist: set rapidly to floor in a two-handed dribble.
2. Teach use of hands and wrist: set the ball to the wall and receive it directly (set from several inches away from wall, and then several feet from wall). Set the ball to the wall, let the ball bounce once, and set back to wall.
3. Underhand set to self.
4. Overhand set to self (stay in specified area).
5. Alternate underhand and overhand set to self.
6. Move under ball, touch right or left knee to floor, come up, and set to self.
7. Overhand set to self: turn 180° or 360°, set.
8. Overhand set to self: sit, stand up, and set.
9. Overhand set to self: lie on floor, stand up, and set.
10. Overhand set to self: sit on floor, set to self, stand up and set to self.
11. Set to self: let bounce, backset to self, repeat.
12. Jump set to self or jump set to wall. To aid in proper timing, players call out "up," and "set" as they execute these skills. Setter may also clap hands in the air, then set the ball.
13. Zig-zag overhand set over net. Follow path of ball by moving under the net. Set five times along net.

MAXIM: *Players must spend time outside of practice training on their own. Success in the final analysis is determined by the individual.*

Set Series—Single Contact 2's

Purpose: Set and movement training.

Individual Goal: Ten good sets.

Description: Partners perpendicular to net, about 15 feet apart. One player tosses ball while other performs drill. After ten good sets change tasks, or if skill level warrants, both players perform drill alternately.

1. Set to partner, sit, stand up, and receive set from partner.
2. Set to partner, push-up position, stand up, receive set.
3. Set to partner, turn 360°, receive set.
4. Set to partner, roll, stand up, and receive set.
5. Rejection: if partner turns away from you, you must self set until partner faces you and accepts the set.

MAXIM: *Convince me that you are striving for perfection.*

Set Series—Two Contacts—2's

Purpose: Set technique training.

Goal: Three sets of 20. If error is made drill begins over at zero.

Description: Partners perpendicular to net, about 15 feet apart.

1. Set to self, 180° turn, backset to partner.
2. Set to self, sit, stand, set to partner.
3. Set to self, squat-thrust, stand, set to partner.
4. Set to self, 90° turn (alternate to right and left side), underhand set to partner.
5. Set to self, jump set to partner.
6. Set to self, let bounce, set to partner.
7. Set to self, 360° turn, set to partner.

MAXIM: *Maximum effort must be made to set every ball even under difficult circumstances. Valuable practice time can best be utilized by making an attempt for every ball.*

Two-Ball Drills—2's (Figures 2-7, 2-8, 2-9, 2-10)

Purpose: Set and movement training.

Goal: Specific time period.

Description: Partners perpendicular to net about 15 feet apart. Each partner has one ball.

1. Simultaneous underhand sets back and forth. Partners set ball high and low or parallel.
2. Simultaneous overhand sets.
3. Set and soccer kick (Figure 2-7).
4. Set and two-hand roll (Figure 2-8).

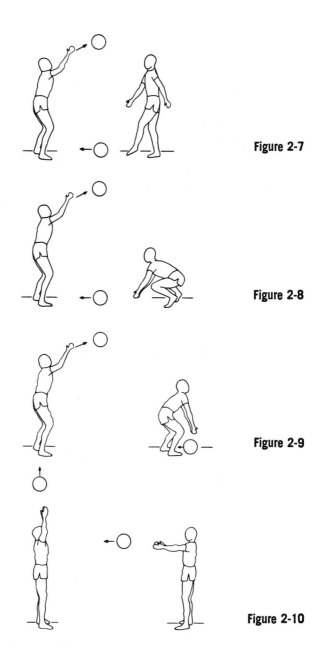

Figure 2-7

Figure 2-8

Figure 2-9

Figure 2-10

5. Set and turn backwards, hike position, roll ball between legs (Figure 2-9).
6. Self set, catch ball thrown from partner to chest height area as set is in air, throw back to partner, set ball in air, and so on. Can use different weight balls to catch (Figure 2-10).

Jump Sets—2's

Purpose: Jump set training and conditioning.

Group Goal: Three sets of 20. If ball drops or error is made, drill begins again at zero.

Description: Partners jump set low and quick over net. Ball is set just high enough to go over the net, with players jumping as high as possible. Three sets of 20. On the third set of 20, jump set to self, then jump set to partner.

MAXIM: *Help eliminate cliques and enhance team cohesion by assigning partners and groups in drills.*

Jog and Set—2's

Purpose: Set technique and movement training, warmup.

Goal: Specific time period.

Description:

1. Partners facing one another, one jogs forward while the other jogs backwards. Stop and set to partner and continue jogging. All players moving in the same direction around the gym.
2. Partners jog forward. The forward player looks back for the pass and the rear player then passes ball over partner's head who then backsets. When coach indicates, change tasks. Stress good peripheral vision, seeing other teammates' movement around gym.

Find Ball and Set—2's

Purpose: Set technique, spatial orientation.

Individual Goal: Ten good sets.

Description: Partners perpendicular to net, one positioned near the net and one on the endline. Both players face away from the net. Player at net calls out partner's name and immediately tosses ball into the air. Partner turns, finds ball, squares off to the target, and sets ball back to partner. After ten good sets change tasks. *Variation:* Frontcourt player bounces ball hard on floor to rebound near receiver and calls out receiver's name. Receiver faces away from net. When receiver hears name called, player quickly turns, finds ball, and sets back to partner. After ten good sets change tasks.

Sideline to Sideline Sets—2's

Purpose: Set technique training, distance work.

Individual Goal: 25 good sideline to sideline sets.

Description: Partners parallel to net about 10 feet apart. Partners practice high sets back and forth, taking one step back after each set, until partners are setting sideline to sideline. After 25 good sideline-to-sideline sets, players take one step forward after each set until they are in original starting position. Stress knee bend, simultaneous arm and leg extension, and follow-through.

MAXIM: *Continually remind players of the importance of performing skills correctly. Completion of the drill and proper technique are the goals in all drills.*

Set and Count—2's

Purpose: Set technique training combined with mental skills.

Goal: Specific time period.

Description: Partners perpendicular to net about 15 feet apart. A sets to partner, looks across to partner, and calls out the number of fingers held up on one hand. Immediately after A sets ball, partner holds up fingers for the count. Continuous setting and counting. *Advanced Variations:* 1) Hold two hands up and add numbers. 2) Hold two hands up and multiply.

MAXIM: *Drills must make players react quickly, both mentally and physically.*

MAXIM: *Setters must have good peripheral vision and be able to quickly look away from the ball before and after the set task.*

Set and Cover—2's

Purpose: Set technique training and cover work.

Goal: Specific time period.

Description: Partners perpendicular to net about 15 feet apart. Set to partner and cover (move a few feet to either the right, the left, or turn and cover behind you as you would do after a backset), then quickly move back to your original position to receive the set back from partner. Continuous setting with both players covering after each set. Stress that in the game after every set, players must cover the attacker. *Advanced Variation:* Set to partner, move to within a few feet of partner, and cover to the right or left. Partner self sets once in between and then sets back to partner in original position. Cover ten times and change tasks.

MAXIM: Each drill must serve a specific purpose and that purpose is a step-by-step progression leading to the game.

Set and Backpedal—2's

Purpose: Set technique and movement training.

Individual Goal: Ten good sets.

Description: Partners perpendicular to net, one positioned near net, one on endline. Player at net sets ball high and near midcourt. Endline player moves forward, sets ball back to partner, quickly backpedals to a position behind the endline, and quickly returns to midcourt to receive next pass from partner. For beginners, player at net may self set once in between. After ten good sets change tasks. Stress playing the ball in front of the body, and using entire body when accelerating into the set.

Bounce Set Series—2's

Purpose: Set technique training, warmup, fun.

Individual Goal: Ten good sets.

Description: Partners perpendicular to net, one positioned near the net and one sitting on the endline. Player at net bounces the ball off the floor toward endline player. As ball bounces, endline player stands up, moves to ball, sets ball to partner, and returns to start position. After ten good sets change tasks. Repeat drill varying the starting positions, for example, push-up position, sitting position, lying on back, crab position, facing away from net, and so on. Vary the direction and height of bounce as players reach higher skill levels.

Corner Sets—2's

Purpose: Backcourt set training.

Goal: Specific time period.

Description: One stationary player positioned at the corner of the net and the other player diagonally across in the backcourt. Stationary player passes ball high or low to receiver in various positions in the backcourt. Backcourt player overhand sets high to partner at net. Continuous frontcourt pass and backcourt setting. Stress the importance of the backcourt player calling "mine" prior to each set.

MAXIM: To some extent, the quality of the attack depends on the quality of the set.

Set and Run Series—2's

Purpose: Set and movement training, warmup, and conditioning.

Individual Goal: Good sets and hard work for 30 seconds.

Description: Partners parallel to net. Player *A* is on the sideline and Player *B* at midcourt.

1. Player *B* sets to player *A*. *A* sets to *B* and runs to opposite sideline to receive backset from *B*. Player *A* sets forward to *B* and runs back to original position. Player *A* sets ball forward only. If skill level warrants, *B* may self set the ball and then backset to give player *A* adequate time to get to the ball. Change tasks after 30 seconds.
2. Player *B* sets to *A*, *A* sets to *B*, and runs to the opposite sideline. *B* self sets, turns 180°, and sets to *A* on this side. Change tasks after 30 seconds.
3. Player *B* sets to *A*, *A* sets to *B*, and runs around *B* back to original position. *B* self sets in between and then back to *A*. Change tasks after 30 seconds.
4. Player *B* sets to *A*, *A* hits ball back to *B*, and runs around *B* back to original position. *B* digs ball up, self sets, and sets back to partner. Change tasks after 30 seconds.

MAXIM: *No matter how inaccurate the pass or how difficult it appears, in practice always make the attempt to overhand set every ball.*

Mini-Shuttle with Cover—3's (Figure 2-11)

Purpose: Set technique training and cover work.

Goal: Specific time period.

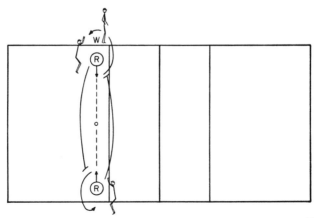

Figure 2-11

Description: Groups of three parallel to the net near the sidelines. Two players lined up one behind the other on one sideline, one player on the opposite side. The drill begins with the line of two players. Set, move forward to the right, cover, and remain on the opposite side. Stress quick movement to the ball and setting from a balanced position. Continuous set and cover.

MAXIM: *Many errors in technique can be avoided when proper footwork is stressed.*

Front- and Backset Series—3's

Purpose: Set technique training, front and backsets.

Individual Goal: Timed one minute.

Description: Players A and B on opposite sidelines, C at midcourt.

1. A sets to C who backsets to B. C turns around to receive set from B and backsets to A. Change tasks after one minute.
2. A sets to C who backsets to B. B crosscourt sets to A. Change tasks after one minute.
3. Players B and C face player A. Player A sets to C, C jump sets ball back to A, A sets crosscourt to B, B crosscourt sets back to A. A jump sets to C, C jump sets back to A, A sets across to B. Change tasks after one minute.

Front- and Backset Series—3's—Two Balls

Purpose: Set technique training, front- and backsets.

Goal: Timed one minute.

Description: Players A and C on opposite sidelines, B midcourt.

1. A and C start with a ball. A sets to B and B front sets ball back to A. Simultaneously as A sets to B, C self-sets ball and then sets to B who has turned to face C. Change tasks after one minute.
2. Players A and C start with a ball. Simultaneously player A sets to B and C sets across to A. B then backsets to C. Change tasks after one minute.

Frontsets—3's—Two Balls (Figure 2-12)

Purpose: Front set training, straight and diagonal.

Goal: Timed 30 seconds.

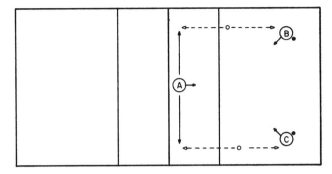

Figure 2-12

Description: Player A positioned at center front with back to net, player B right back, player C left back. Backcourt players each begin with one ball. Player A receives the set from B and sets the ball straight back to B. Player A then moves quickly to a position opposite C and receives the set from C and sets straight back. Backcourt players self set once after receiving the ball from A. Repeat drill with player A center back and players B and C left and right front. Players B and C set the ball diagonally back to player A (at left or right back), and player A sets diagonally across to the corner of the net as would occur in the game. Players B and C self set after they receive the backcourt set. Change tasks after 30 seconds.

Triangle Sets—3's

Purpose: Set training, squaring off to the target.

Goal: Timed one minute.

Description: Players positioned ten to 15 feet apart and form a triangle. Players set back and forth working on good positioning prior to the pass, and squaring off to the target. When space permits, players should be positioned in court-related positions—center front, center back, and right or left front positions. After one minute change tasks.

MAXIM: *Drills must make players move; very rarely does the ball come directly to you.*

Triangle Sets—3's—Two Balls (Figure 2-13)

Purpose: Front- and backset training with short time span between sets.

Goal: Timed one minute.

Description: Players A, B and C are positioned in a triangle as in diagram. Balls start with players A and C. Simultaneously C sets to A and A

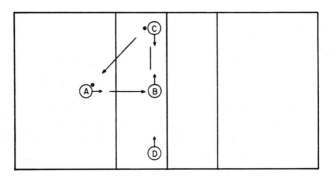

Figure 2-13

sets to *B*. Players continue to set counter-clockwise in this triangle. Player *B* concentrates on setting the ball high and about one foot from the net and from the sideline. The drill is repeated with players forming this triangle to the opposite side (*D*). Balls start with players *A* and *D*. *D* sets to *A* and *A* sets to *B* simultaneously. Player *B* now backsets the ball to *D*. Players continue to set clockwise in the triangle. Change tasks after one minute.

Triangle Sets—3's—Two Balls (Figure 2-14)

Purpose: Frontset training with short time span between sets.

Goal: Timed one minute.

Description: Players positioned in a triangle as in diagram. Balls start with players *A* and *D*. Simultaneous with *D*'s set to *A*, *A* sets to *C*. *A* continues to set one ball back to *D* and the other ball back to *C*. Change tasks after one minute.

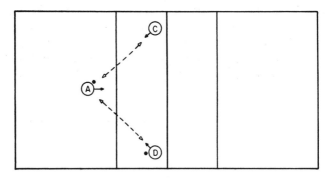

Figure 2-14

Set From Free Ball Pass—4's (Figure 2-15)

Purpose: Free ball pass and set training.

Individual Goal: Specific time period.

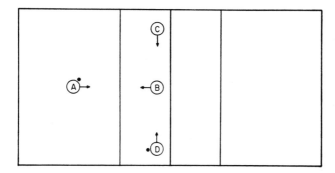

Figure 2-15

Description: Groups of four players positioned as in diagram. Player *B* begins drill with underhand toss to *A*. *A* passes ball overhand or underhand back to *B*, who sets ball either forward or back to *C* or *D*, who passes ball back to *A*. Continuous pass and set work. Players rotate positions after a specific time period. The drill may be repeated with two setters alternating the setting task at position *B*. Each in turn would set, cover, and move to the right back area just behind the ten-foot line (6-2 defensive position). It is important that setters keep eyes forward on opponents and do not turn their back to the net when moving to the right back area. *C* and *D* may call out type of set they would like to receive.

MAXIM: *The set should be practiced as quickly as possible in combination with the pass (see Chapter 1).*

MAXIM: *The setter must learn to deal with balls passed low, high, and close to the net. The setter must learn to set while standing, running, jumping, rolling, and turning.*

Set From Free Ball Pass—4's—Two Balls (Figure 2-15)

Purpose: Free ball pass and set training with short time span between sets.

Goal: Specific time period.

Description: Groups of four players, positioned as in diagram. Balls start with players *A* and *D*. Player *A* passes to *B* while *D* sets to *A*. Player *B* sets the first pass forward to *C* and backsets the next ball to *D*. Players *D* and *C* continue to direct the ball back to *A*, while *B* alternates setting one ball forward and the next ball back. Change tasks after one minute.

Set and Move—4's—Two Balls (Figure 2-16)

Purpose: Set training with movement with short time span between sets.

Goal: Specific time period.

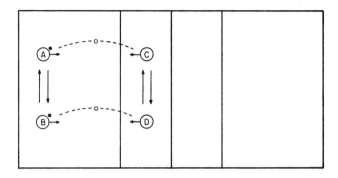

Figure 2-16

Description: Players positioned about 15 feet apart and forming a rectangle. Balls start with backcourt players *A* and *B*. *A* and *B* simultaneously set forward directly across to partner. After setting, players *A* and *B* switch positions. Frontcourt players *C* and *D* set balls directly back, then they also switch positions. Players continuously set ball directly forward and change positions with player next to them. If skill level warrants, only one group of players changes places with the remaining pair stationary.

MAXIM: *Continually reinforce good technique. Provide encouragement and support.*

Frontcourt and Backcourt Sets (Figure 2-17)

Purpose: Set technique training inside ten-foot line area.

Group Goal: Two players must accurately set five balls high to the outside attacker.

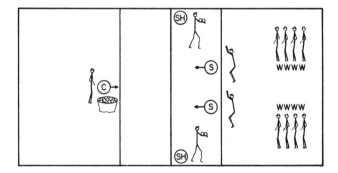

Figure 2-17

Description: Two receivers within ten-foot line area. Two players in target position at the corners of the net to catch sets. Coach on opposite side of the net. The coach tosses the ball anywhere in the ten-foot line area for either receiver to set, not necessarily alternating tosses. The coach hits the net purposely to see if receivers are using forward footwork. Receivers set the ball high to the corner of the net. Five good sets by the team of receivers and they become the set targets, targets become shaggers, shaggers move into the receiving line. New group moves forward into drill. *Variation:* Two receivers in backcourt. Coach tosses ball anywhere behind ten-foot line area. Receiver calls "mine" and sets high to the outside attacker diagonally across. *Variation:* (Figure 2-18). Three players start at wall (or other object if wall is too far from endline) opposite the center back area of the court. The coach tosses the ball anywhere on the court. The first receiver in line overhand sets the ball diagonally across to outside attacker, and runs back to touch the wall. While the first receiver is running back, receivers two and three take their turns. After ten good sets the setter becomes a set target (shagger at corner). As each individual completes a drill, a new player rotates in so drill is continuous.

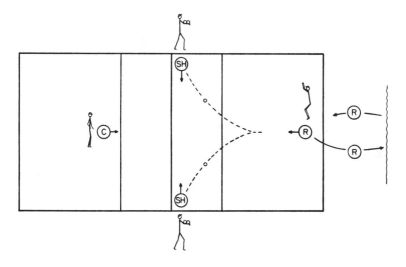

Figure 2-18

MAXIM: *Off deep sets, set the on-hand attacker (right side for leftys, left side for right-handers). This is the easier attack position off a deep set.*

Crosscourt Sets (Figure 2-19)

Purpose: Set technique training, distance work, crosscourt setting, warmup.

Goal: Specific time period.

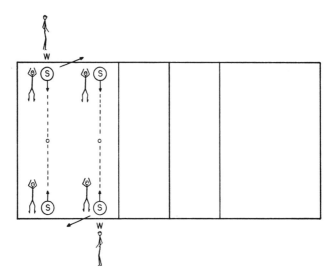

Figure 2-19

Description: Groups of six, one group on each side of the net. Players overhand set ball high to opposite sideline, then move to adjacent line. For beginners, self set, then set across. To strengthen hands, wrists, and forearms for setting this distance, partner work may be done setting a weighted volleyball, a basketball, or soccer ball.

MAXIM: *Move quickly to the ball, stop, and set from a balanced position.*

Crosscourt Sets Around Chair (Figure 2-20)

Purpose: Set technique training, crosscourt sets.

Team Goal: 50 good crosscourt sets.

Description: One line of players near the right sideline and one line near left sideline. One chair placed in front of each line, on the intersection of the sideline and ten foot line. First player in each line moves around the chair and back into the court to set the ball crosscourt (moving around the chair forces players to start near sideline for full crosscourt setting). Follow set and cover, then move to the end of the opposite line. Continuous crosscourt sets. For beginners, who have difficulty setting the full crosscourt distance, use self-set and then set crosscourt.

MAXIM: *Make players believe they can make the changes you want. Do not reinforce their uncertainty.*

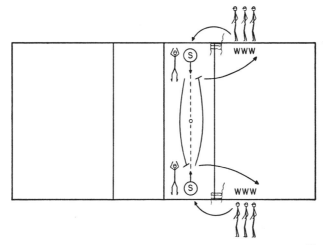

Figure 2-20

Set Series—Coach Bounce or Toss (Figure 2-21)

Purpose: Set technique and accuracy training.

Goal: Specific time period.

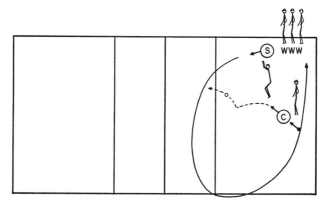

Figure 2-21

Description: A line of setters positioned in right back area of the court, coach midcourt on the same side of the net. The coach bounces or tosses the ball forward and the first setter in line releases (as in the 6-2 offense) to the frontcourt to set the ball. The setter follows the set, covers, remains for one turn in the corner position at the net as a target, runs, hands ball to the coach, and returns to the end of the set line. Coach varies the direction and height of the bounce or toss. Repeat drill with setters on left side.

Progression:

1. High set foward or jump set.
2. High backset or jump set.
3. Alternate high set forward and back.
4. High set forward or back as indicated by the coach just prior to the set. It is important to maintain a balanced up and down posture that allows you to set in either direction.

MAXIM: *Coach challenges the setter by varying the position and difficulty of the pass.*

MAXIM: *Setters must disguise the direction of the set until the last moment.*

MAXIM: *A setter's obligation is to set with pinpoint accuracy to enhance the attacker's performance.*

Set Series—Two Balls (Figure 2-22)

Purpose: Front and backset training.

Goal: Specific time period.

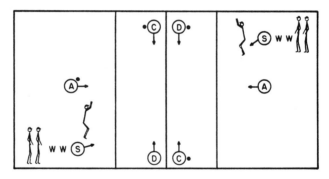

Figure 2-22

Description:

1. For frontsets: One stationary player left front (*C*), and center back (*A*) and a line of three or more setters coming from right back. Balls start with players *A* and *C*. Player *A* tosses the ball forward to the net between zones two and three and the first setter *D* moves forward to set the ball forward to player *C*. As *A* is tossing, player *C* tosses another ball to *A*. The first setter sets the ball and returns to the end of the set line.

2. For backsets: One stationary player right front (D) and center back (A). Setters now backset each ball.
3. Alternating front- and backsets: Stationary players right front (D), left front (C) and center back (A), and one line of setters right back. It is best to have an odd number of setters so setters will alternate front and backsets each turn. Balls start with players D and C. Player C begins with a toss to A, who passes forward for the first setter to release and set forward. As A is passing, player D passes another ball to A. Player A passes the ball forward for the second setter to backset. Each setter in turn releases to the front court sets and returns to the end of the set line. Each setter alternates set direction setting opposite that of the previous setter.

Set Shuttle Series (Figure 2-23)

Purpose: Set technique training, backcourt and crosscourt sets, warm-up.

Team Goal: Complete the series. 15 good sets to the right front corner, 15 good sets to the left front corner, 15 good crosscourt sets. The ultimate goal is to complete the series without the ball's ever touching the floor.

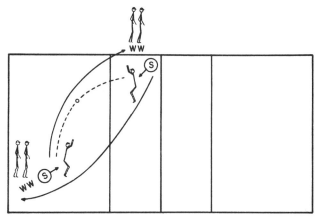

Figure 2-23

Description: Two groups, one on each side of the net, with a minimum of five players in each group. Each group is divided into two lines positioned diagonally on the court corner to corner. The first player in the frontcourt line passes the ball to a position midcourt and the first player in the backcourt line moves forward to set the ball high to the corner of the net. After contact, each player moves to the left and to the end of the opposite line. The frontcourt players generally underhand pass the ball while the backcourt overhand sets the ball (may repeat with backcourt underhand set). Continuous set and pass without letting the ball touch the floor. When the goal of 15 good sets to the frontcourt is achieved, without stopping or dropping the ball reposition players to set to the opposite corner. Complete 15 good sets and reposition lines to set crosscourt, sideline to sideline.

MAXIM: *In practice and in the game, never let the ball hit the floor without making an attempt for it.*

Shuttle with Backset (Figure 2-24)

Purpose: Set technique training, backsets, crosscourt sets, warmup.

Team Goal: 50 good backsets.

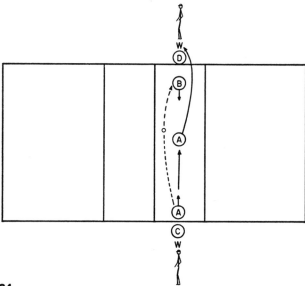

Figure 2-24

Description: Two groups, one on each side of the net. Groups with a minimum of seven players each are divided into two lines positioned opposite one another, parallel to and about five feet away from the net. The first player in each line is positioned on the sideline. Player *A* sets the ball crosscourt to player *B* and moves forward to the middle of the court to receive a set from *B*. Player *A* backsets the ball to player *C* and moves forward to the right and to the end of the opposite line. Player *C* sets across to *D* and moves forward, then receives pass from *D* and backsets. This drill may be added to the set shuttle series.

Set Shuttle—Two Balls (Figure 2-25)

Purpose: Set technique training, backcourt sets, warmup, fun.

Team Goal: Specific time period.

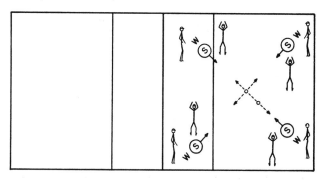

Figure 2-25

Description: Two groups, one on each side of the net. Each group, with a minimum of eight players in each group, is divided into four lines positioned diagonally on the court corner to corner. Two balls start at approximately the same time from the right and left back lines. Players set diagonally across to opposite line and after set rotate to their right to the end of the adjacent line. It is important that the backcourt player set the ball high and to the corner of the net. Frontcourt players set to a position in the back half of the court.

MAXIM: *Practice must be enjoyable to do any good.*

Set From Backcourt Dig—6-2 System (Figure 2-26)

Purpose: Set training from backcourt dig.

Goal: Specific time period.

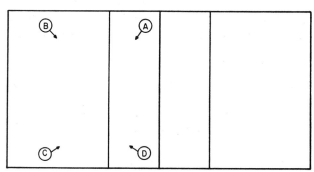

Figure 2-26

Description: Four players on one side of the court, *D* positioned at right front, *C* right back, *A* left front and *B* left back. Player *A* sets across to *D* who hits to *B*. *B* digs the ball forward for *C* to release to the front court to set. *C* sets across to *A* and the sequence is repeated. This simulates the game situation with the backcourt setter releasing to set the dug ball, then returning for the next defensive play. If the ball is dug too far from the setter, another player must step in to set. Drill is repeated with *A* hitting to *C* and *B* releasing to set. This could occur in the game when the backcourt setter digs the first ball.

Basketball Accuracy Set Contest (Figure 2-27)

Purpose: Set technique and accuracy training, warmup and conditioning.

Goal: First to score 15 points wins.

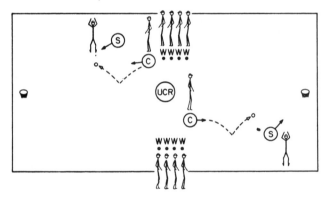

Figure 2-27

Description: A regulation basketball court may be used, but a smaller court is preferred if available. Two coaches are the tossers. Players are in two lines positioned to the right and slightly behind the coaches (drill should also be done from the left). The first player in each line hands the ball to the coach, who bounces the ball in the direction of the basket. On the rebound the player overhand sets the ball to the basket. Players shag ball and move to the end of the next line. Each player in turn hands the coach the ball prior to their turn. Two points are scored for a basket (sets off the backboard do not count), and one for hitting the rim. The first player to win 15 points wins.

MAXIM: *Bounce pass simulates the timing and trajectory of the game pass.*

Volley-Basketball Set Contest (Figure 2-28)

Purpose: Set training.

Goal: First to score 21 points wins.

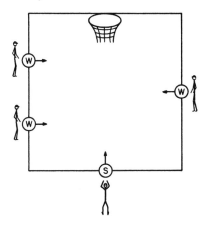

Figure 2-28

Description: One player starts at the free-throw line, with remaining players outside the key area. The player at the free-throw line tosses the ball and sets to the basket. Two points are scored for a swish, and one point if the ball touches the rim and goes in. If the shot is missed, any player may overhand set the next ball on the fly or on the first bounce. The first player to call for the ball is entitled to set the ball. All sets made from this position are worth two points (sets off the backboard do not count). Any number of overhand set attempts may be made while the ball can be played off the fly or on one bounce. When this is not possible, play begins over at free throw line by a new setter. The first player to score 21 points wins.

MAXIM: *Make practices interesting and fun with some less disciplined drills.*

 # The Attack

The attack is the primary offensive weapon and its purpose is to score points. The attack encompasses a variety of options. The less one's height and jumping ability, the more important it is to use the attack options in order to be an effective hitter. The wider the range of attack options, the more difficult it is for opposing front- and backcourt defensive players to receive the ball. The attacker must disguise the attack option as long as possible for best results. The attack option is determined by attacker capabilities, height, positioning of the block, and positioning of the set.

ATTACK OPTIONS

Power Attack

Attacking the ball with maximum power, around, through, or off the block. On the outside set, the ball may be directed crosscourt or down the line. On the middle set, the ball may be directed to the power angle or cut back across the body to the opposite side.

Dink/Tip

After establishing power and the defense is dug in, the ball is tapped softly over the blocker's hands. The tip is generally used on balls set close or one to two feet off the net. The hand is open and contact is made on the pads of the fingers. Follow through just enough to place the ball to the target. The tip should be learned with both the right and left hand. With the ability to use either hand, many wide sets can be kept in play. This is one of the easiest yet most effective attack variations. The tip is a psychological weapon as this soft attack often embarrasses opponents who feel that this easy attack should be playable, but often is not.

Soft/Off-Speed

Used to change the pace of the game and to catch the defense off guard. Placement is emphasized more than speed. Contact and follow-through is primarily a wrist snap action with the hand rolling over the top of the ball, imparting topspin. The center of the court is a vulnerable spot for

68

this attack. The off-speed shot may be used on balls set close or those deep off the net.

Deep Corners

Hit the corners deep crosscourt or down the line. This allows a shorter player to effectively hit around or off the top of a taller block. The deep hit is an effective option for balls set five to 10 feet off the net, as well as for the attack by back row players. The corners are vulnerable attack spots, not only because they are difficult to cover, but because they force the player to question whether close balls are in or out. Emphasis is placed on good hand contact, wrist snap, and placement.

Sharp Angle/Line

The sharp angle attack is used when balls are set close to the net or when the block is covering the line area. The ball is hit at an extreme angle inside the block, directed in front of the 10-foot line or between the front- and backcourt receivers. To execute the sharp angle shot, dip the shoulder nearest to the net and use wrist and forearm action to cut the ball inside the block. The ball is hit down the line when the blocker moves inside to cover for the angle attack. The attacker utilizes the same approach and then turns in the air to hit the power attack down the line. For quickness and deception, the armswing begins first and the body rotation follows.

Hole in Block

The attacker can hit through a poorly positioned double or triple block. The attacker must develop a feel for the block and know in which situations the block might not be solid. The attacker should learn to perceive block movement and look for the hole in the block.

Off the Block (Wipe-Off/Tool)

When the ball is set close to the net and near the sideline the attacker can sweep the ball off the blocker's hands and out of bounds. The attacker must contact the side of the ball, hitting it partially into the block and following through out of bounds. The ball may be hit hard or tipped off the block.

Rebound Play

When the attacker is trapped and cannot hit around the block, tap the ball directly into the block and play the ball up as it rebounds back.

Roundhouse

Ball contact behind head with sidearm motion. Contact is made on bottom portion of ball with quick wrist action imparting topspin.

THE APPROACH

A good approach is essential for an effective vertical jump and in turn an effective attack. The most common approaches are the step-hop approach and the step-close approach. The selection of the style of approach depends on personal preference, but can also be dictated by the situation. Players should learn to execute the attack with no approach, as well as with a short and longer step approach. For most approaches, the player begins about ten to 15 feet from the net and waits until the ball is set high to determine its trajectory and placement. The attacker jumps into the air at an arm's distance behind the ball. The approach is quick, smooth, and vigorous, and is synchronized with the arm swing for maximum lift. The movement is continuous from start to jump recovery. The greater the ability of the legs to withstand the abrupt change from forward to upward with the least significant stoppage, the greater the jumping ability. The approach pattern for right handers is at a 45° angle from the left and center front positions and straight in on the right side. This approach allows the attacker both line and crosscourt power attack options because moving the hand, arm, and shoulder from right to left (reversed for left-handed players) is the easiest and most powerful move. It is recommended that the footwork for the approach be taught first, independently of the arms.

Step-Hop Approach Checklist (Figure 3-1)

1. Medium-high track-start ready position.
2. One or two running steps forward prior to the hop.
3. Lift both feet and jump-hop landing on both feet.
4. Land with feet 1½ to 2 feet apart and on the heels, rocking to the toes into the jump.
5. During the hop forward the arms go back. Simultaneously as the heels contact the ground, the arms drive down and up, lifting the body.

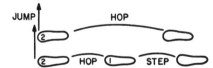

Figure 3-1

Three-Step Step-Close Approach Checklist (Figure 3-2)

1. Medium-high track-start position.

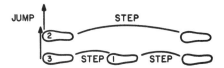

Figure 3-2

2. First step is a short running step forward with left foot for right handers and right foot for left handers. This is a timing or reading step
   helping the attacker get to the proper spot at the proper time.
3. The second step is a breaking step landing on the heel. The third step
   is a closing step landing on the toe.
4. The timing is step, heel-toe (step-close), with the closing step made
   as quickly as possible after the last running step.
5. On the second step the arms go back and on the last step they drive
   down and up, lifting the body.

Four-Step Step-Close Approach Checklist (Figure 3-3)

1. Medium high track-start position.
2. First step is a short running step forward with left foot for left handers
   and right foot for right handers. This is a timing or reading step
   helping the attacker get to the proper spot at the proper time.
3. The second step is longer; the third step is a breaking step landing on
   the heel; the fourth step is a closing step landing on the toe.
4. The timing is step, run, heel-toe (step-close), with the player accelerating into the approach. The closing steps are made as quickly
   as possible after the last running step.
5. On the third step as the foot goes forward the arms go back. On the
   last step the arms drive down and up, lifting the body.

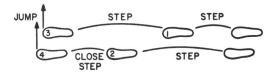

Figure 3-3

ATTACK CHECKLIST (Figure 3-4)

Coordination of Approach and Jump

1. Prior to the last step or hop the arms swing down and back as far as
   possible, with the upper body tilted forward.
2. On the last step or hop the body is coiled like a spring, knees flexed
   about 120°, trunk flexed forward, nonhitting shoulder toward net.
3. Immediately on the last step or hop, momentum abruptly changes
   from forward to upward.

Figure 3-4

4. Hands lead, arms move quickly and vigorously forward and upward, keeping arms close to body.
5. Back arched while ascending, shoulders rotated back.
6. Hitting arm is in a throwing position with the non-hitting hand pointing at the ball.
7. Throw hitting arm up at ball and snap; non-hitting hand pulls down.
8. Contact on palm of open hand.
9. Use quick, compact snapping motion.

Contact (Figure 3-5)

All attack options are similar until the point of contact. The "ready position" of the body and arm prior to contact are all similar and allow for maximum deception and choice of option.

Figure 3-5   1.   2.   3.   4.

For Power Attack

1. Wrist hyperextended back and flexible prior to contact.

2. Arm and wrist uncoil and snap quickly upward and forward into the ball.
3. Contact is made in front of the body over the hitting shoulder at almost maximum arm reach, shoulder extended up.
4. Contact is made with the entire hand (open or slightly cupped). Contact on the palm gives the power while the fingers wrap around the ball for control and direction.
5. Arm follows through on same side of body. Attacker changes course of ball by changing body position in air to face direction of attack.
6. Body snaps forward, fingers pointed downward after contact.

For Deception and Quick Change of Direction

Use quick turn with forearm and wrist hitting across the body for less power but more deception.

For Soft/Off-Speed Attack

Similar to power attack but arm not swung through with such force. Ball may be hit upward with use of topspin.

Dink/Tip

As the arm uncoils the motion is slowed just prior to contact. The hand is open and contact is made on the pads of the fingers. The hand guides the ball softly to the desired target, with very little wrist action.

Landing

Cushion jump recovery by landing on both feet and bending the knees.

Drills

It is recommended that the approach and attack skills be taught independently of one another and combined later. This complex skill can be practiced in its entirety to give players a feel for what they are learning, but progressions should be utilized later to teach, emphasize, and correct proper technique. Demonstration of the various portions of the attack skill must be shown slowly so the eye can see and understand the skill parts. It is also recommended that the attack be taught on a lower net and gradually raised as skill level warrants.

Hit Stationary Ball

Purpose: To emphasize contact and wrist snap.

Goal: Specific time period.

Description: Coach stands on chair on same side of net as players and holds ball about one to two feet above net. Players hit ball out of coach's hand (first using the last step of the approach, then adding the complete approach). Coach pulls hand away at moment attacker hits ball. With the ball stationary, the attacker can completely concentrate on technique.

Approach Overline (Figure 3-6)

Purpose: Running approach with long last step.

Goal: Specific time period.

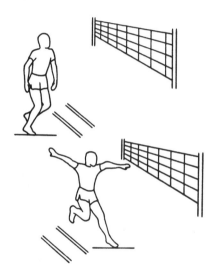

Figure 3-6

Description: Place tape marks about one to two feet apart in the approach runway at the net. The player must jump over this taped section, land, and quickly jump up for the attack. Stress a long step and running rather than walking into the approach. A small mat could be used instead of the tape.

Approach and Catch

Purpose: Attack timing.

Goal: Specific time period.

Description: Coach tosses ball, player approaches, jumps, and catches ball at its peak with two hands. Ball must be caught above the height of the net, as the ball must be contacted above the net for a successful attack.

Approach, Catch, and Throw

Purpose: Attack timing.

Goal: Specific time period.

Description: Coach tosses ball, player approaches, jumps, catches, and throws ball down into opponent's court with both hands. This catch and throw simulates the "hang time" necessary to attack the ball in the air. Catch and throw the ball quickly while the body is at its highest position in the air. Snap wrists, arms, and body forward, simulating the attack action.

Coach Toss for Quick Attack

Purpose: Approach and attack training.

Goal: Specific time period.

Description: Player approaches for quick attack at a position about one foot from the coach. Player jumps into air before toss and the coach must time toss to attacker's jump. The attacker is able to concentrate primarily on the approach and hit.

Coach Toss for Short Set

Purpose: Approach and attack training.

Goal: Specific period of time.

Description: Coach tosses low set two to three feet above net for player to attack. The short set is easier to time because players may release for the approach shortly after the ball is set.

Coach Toss for Oversets

Purpose: Overset work.

Goal: Specific period of time.

Description: Coach tosses from opponent's side of court for player to hit as if opponents had overset.

Coach Toss for Attack, Backpedal, Attack. . .

Purpose: Attack transition.

Individual Goal: 3–4 trips.

Description: Coach tosses three in a row for each attacker. Hit, backpedal, hit, backpedal, hit. *Variation*: Coach tosses anywhere, high or low, at ten-foot line, or over the net. If ball is tossed over the net, player must block. Attacker practices adjusting for various types of sets, as well as quick transition for many hits in succession.

Model Approaches Around Gym

Purpose: Approach work.

Individual Goal: 15 approaches.

Description: Jog slowly or walk around gym. On whistle command, approach and mock attack in air.

MAXIM: *Be specific and concise in error correction. Describe the error and how to correct it.*

Model Approaches at Wall

Purpose: Discourage floating on approach.

Individual Goal: Ten approaches.

Description: Stand ten to 15 feet from a wall, facing wall. Practice the approach moving toward the wall.

Model Approaches with Backpedal

Purpose: Transition and approach work.

Individual Goal: 15 approaches.

Description: Jog slowly or walk around gym. On whistle command, quickly backpedal three steps, approach, and mock attack in air.

Handball Attack at Wall

Purpose: Upper body attack technique.

Individual Goal: Start with ten consecutive standing hits and progress to ten consecutive jumping hits.

Description: Stand about ten feet from the wall and hit the ball downward with a forearm and wrist snap action causing the ball to hit close to your feet and rebound high on the wall. As the ball comes off the wall, reach up to the ball, and using a spike action, hit the ball again to the floor.

Partner Attack Warmup

Purpose: Shoulder warmup, upper body attack technique.

Goal: Five minute routine, about five repetitions of each skill.

Description: Partners perpendicular to net, one near the net and one on endline.

1. Two hands above head, throw to partner.
2. One hand above head, throw to partner.
3. Two hands above head, throw ball to floor, ball bounces midcourt and rebounds near partner's sideline. Emphasize use of good body snap.
4. One hand above head, throw ball to floor rebounding near partner. Foot position as in attack; no steps taken.
5. Standing hit to partner. Ball bounces midcourt rebounding near partner. Toss ball in air, reach up to ball (should be on tiptoes) and contact ball in front of body. Snap wrist into ball with no additional follow-through. Keep hand open and fingers spread for control and accuracy. Fingers pointed down on contact. Strive for rebound height rather than distance.
6. Two-handed self toss, jump in air, hit ball to floor to rebound near partner.

Approach to Net-Tap-Tap

Purpose: Approach and upper body attack technique and use of non-hitting arm.

Individual Goal: 15 approaches.

Description: Players approach the net, jump and mock attack in air with this variation. Attacker taps top of net first with the nonhitting hand, immediately followed by the hitting hand. Backpedal from net and repeat. Stress use of both arms reaching up on armswing and use of shoulder rotation on attack.

Self Toss Attacks With Partner

Purpose: Attack training.

Individual Goal: Five good hits from each position.

Description: Partners midcourt on opposite sides of the net. One player begins with two-handed self toss, jumps and hits ball over net. Partner shags ball and jumps and hits ball back to partner. Repeat from ten-foot line and from three-foot line.

Mini-Shuttle Attack Warmup—3's

Purpose: Shoulder warmup, upper body attack technique.

Goal: Specific time period.

Description: Groups of three players parallel to net near sidelines. Two players line up one behind the other on one sideline, one player on the opposite side. The drill begins with the line of two players. Perform skills as suggested in partner attack warmup, that is, two-hand throw, one-hand throw, two-hand bounce, one-hand bounce, standing hit, and jump hit. After performing the skill, that player runs to the right and to the position at the opposite sideline.

Approach and Mock Attack at Net

Purpose: Approach angles for attack, warmup.

Goal: Specific time period.

Description: Players assume a ready position to attack from the left, center, or right front positions on either side of the net. Additional players line up behind them. Approach, mock attack, and move to the end of that line. After five approaches in one position, move to the end of a new line.

MAXIM: *Establish a patterned approach. Always approach the ball at the same angle so you do not telegraph your intentions to the blockers.*

Mock Approach—3 Positions (Figure 3-7)

Purpose: Approach angles for attack, warmup.

Goal: Specific time period.

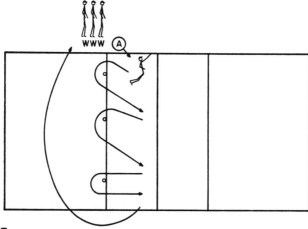

Figure 3-7

Description: Single line on one or both sides of the court. Three balls placed on each court as shown in figure. First player in line approaches at 45° angle from left side of ball and mock attacks at left front position. Backpedal around ball and to left of second ball for mock center attack. Backpedal around ball, and approach to left of third ball. Backpedal around ball and approach straight in for right side attack and move to end of line. Leftys must approach straight in on the first three approaches and at a 45° angle on the right. Players must backpedal quickly away from the net to prepare for the next approach.

Mock Approach With Block (Figure 3-8)

Purpose: Approach angles for attack, proper positioning for block, warmup.

Goal: Specific time period.

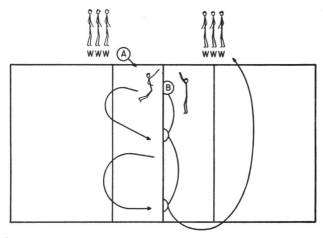

Figure 3-8

Description: Similar to mock approach drill, with the addition of blockers (performed with or without balls on the court). Single line on each side of the court. One side is the attackers, one side is the blockers. The first person in each line assumes proper court position. Attacker mock approaches and attacks from left front, backpedals to about center ten-foot line area, approaches for center attack, backpedals to right, and approaches for right side attack. Blocker must "read" approach and attack direction and position for the one-on-one block. The blocker must jump just after the attacker jumps. The attacker may approach quickly and stop, trying to make the blocker jump prior to the attacker's jump, and then quickly jump as the blocker is on the way down. After three approaches/blocks these two players move to the end of the opposite line and the next two players begin the drill.

MAXIM: *Hard practices build team cohesion.*

Partner Attack Drills

Purpose: Attack technique training, no approach.

Individual Goal: Ten good hits on each new drill.

Description: Partners on same side of net.

1. Attacker near ten-foot line. Partner at net tosses ball for the attack. Step back, opening up to the tosser, use the last step of the approach, hit, and shag. Ten good hits and change tasks.
2. Attacker near three-foot line, with back to net. Partner calls out "ready" and tosses for the attack. Attacker turns, steps back, opens up, uses last step of approach, and hits. Ten good hits and change tasks.
3. Mock block at net, partner tosses ball as player lands, attacker steps back, opens up, uses last step of approach, and hits. Ten good hits and change tasks.

Attack Lines—Attack Options (Figure 3-9)

Purpose: Attack technique training, attack variations, placement, and control.

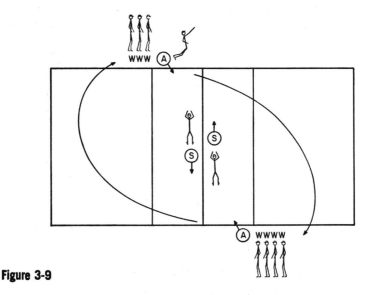

Figure 3-9

Goal: Specific time period.

Description: Two attack lines (right or left sides), one on each side of the net. One setter for each line. Second player in each line tosses ball to setter, first attacker approaches and hits, shags ball, and returns to end of opposite line. Coach verbally designates direction and type of attack to be hit, for example, deep corners, off-speed to center of court, sharp angle, crosscourt, or down the line.

MAXIM: *To be an effective attacker you must utilize many attack variations.*

Attack Lines—Variations (Figure 3-9)

Purpose: Attack training.

Goal: Specific time period.

Variations:

1. Setter sets ball various depths from the net and attacker must adjust accordingly.
2. Setter may set ball high or low, near sideline or inside court. Attacker hits the line on all sideline sets and hits crosscourt on all low or inside sets. Attacker must vary approach speed depending on the type of set.
3. As the attacker makes the approach, the second person in line calls out "line," "angle," or "tip" and the attacker must respond with the correct action.
4. Attacker starts at net, second person in line tosses the ball to setter, attacker backpedals quickly, approaches and hits.
5. Mock block by attacker, second person in line tosses ball to setter just as player lands, backpedals, approaches and hits.
6. Mock block, setter tosses ball to attacker just after landing, attacker passes the ball to the setter, backpedals, approaches, and hits.

After each attack may use designated setters or attacker becomes setter and setter shags ball and moves to the end of the opposite line.

MAXIM: *Attacker must practice making immediate decisions determining the best direction from which to attack the ball.*

MAXIM: *Attackers must change the direction of attack quickly and not telegraph intentions to blockers.*

Attack Lines—Tip Options (Figure 3-10)

Purpose: Tip training.

Goal: Specific time period.

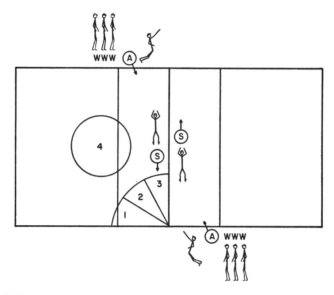

Figure 3-10

Description: Refer to description on previous drill. Tip with the preferred hand to targets one, two, three, or four. Alternate tipping with the right or left hand, depending on the position of the set, using the hand closest to the set. Tip only those balls that can be contacted in front of the body and those set not more than one to two feet from the net.

MAXIM: Never ask a player to do something in the game that you have not worked on in practice.

MAXIM: Do not reveal tip intentions too soon. Be an actor; prepare to attack and at the last moment tip the ball.

Attack—Cover Hitter (Figure 3-11)

Purpose: Set, cover, and attack training.

Team Goal: 25 good hits from the left, center, and right front positions.

Description: One line of tossers, one line of attackers, and a setter. Toss ball to setter, setter sets ball, and both setter and tosser "cover" for the attack. After hit, attacker shags ball and returns to tosser line. Tosser goes to attack line. Change setters as desired. Repeat drill from right and center front positions.

MAXIM: Assume the ball will be blocked and cover.

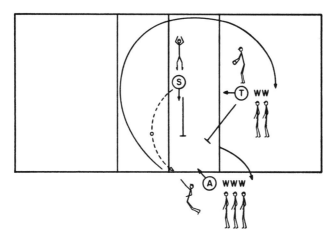

Figure 3-11

Pass, Set, Cover, Attack (Figure 3-12)

Purpose: Pass, set, cover, and attack training.

Team Goal: 25 good hits.

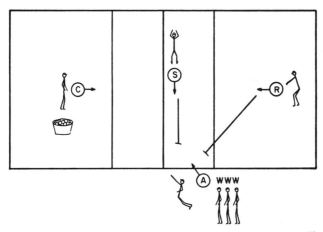

Figure 3-12

Description: One line of receivers midcourt, one line of attackers, a setter, and a tosser (coach) on the opposite side of the net. Coach tosses ball over net to receiver who passes to setter. Setter then sets for attacker. Receiver and setter cover for the attack. Receiver moves to end of attack line, attacker shags ball and returns to reception line.

MAXIM: *Drills should be run quickly and time utilized effectively so there is little standing around.*

Attack From Backcourt Set

Purpose: Attack from backcourt set training.

Team Goal: 50 good hits.

Description: One left-side attack line and one right or center-back set-ting line. Attacker tosses ball back to setter who sets the ball high to the corner of the net. Attacker takes a wide approach and hits crosscourt. Setter covers and returns to attack line. Attacker shags and returns to set line. Stress a wide angle approach for the attacker in order to "open up" to face the court and the setter, rather than looking over the shoulder to see the set. For most right-handed players it is easier to hit the backcourt set from the left front position, so in the game this set is preferred. Repeat drill with right side attack and setting line left back.

MAXIM: *Never refuse any set in practice; you do not have this option in the game.*

Attack From Backcourt Set (Figure 3-13)

Purpose: Attack from backcourt set training.

Team Goal: 50 good hits.

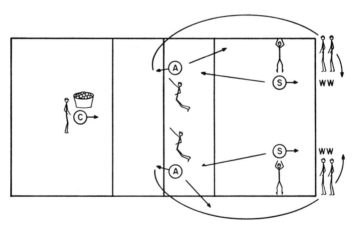

Figure 3-13

Description: Two attackers, one at the right side attack position and the other on the left, facing net and holding net with both hands. Two setters in the backcourt facing away from the court. Coach on opposite side of the net calls "ready" and tosses the ball to backcourt. Attackers back off net while setters turn to find ball. One player calls "mine" and sets diagonally across to attacker and covers. Setter takes place of attacker, attacker shags, and returns to setting line. One new setter moves into the court. Add blockers. *Variation:* Vary starting position of setters, such as sitting, prone, crab position, and so on.

MAXIM: *A fundamental goal in all drills is not only personal achievement but also creating a positive self image.*

Bounce, Set, Attack (Figure 3-14)

Purpose: Attack from backcourt set.

Goal: Specific time period.

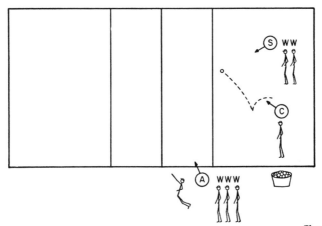

Figure 3-14

Description: One line of attackers hitting at left front and one line of setters starting in the right back position. Coach in center back position bounces the ball forward to rebound behind or in front of the ten-foot line. Setter releases to set, covers attacker, and moves to the end of the attack line. Attacker hits, shags, and moves to the set line. Repeat drill with attackers at right front. Coach varies distance and height of ball rebound.

MAXIM: *Choose your words carefully; it is a very important coaching tool.*

Rapid Hitting (Figure 3-15)

Purpose: Repetitive attack training and conditioning.

Individual Goal: Count the number of good hits out of ten attempts. Coach asks each player the total number of successful hits and the number of consecutive good attacks out of ten.

Team Goal: Group must hit five consecutive good hits to complete the drill.

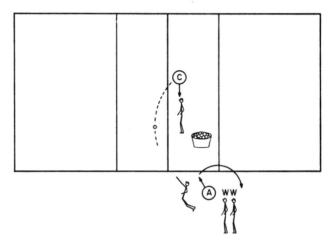

Figure 3-15

Description: Groups of three attackers. Coach tosses, attacker hits ball and moves to the end of the line. Each attacking player receives ten tosses. Remaining players shag.

Variations:

1. Attack high toss from left, center, or right front position.
2. Attack from ten-foot line.
3. Attack quick middle sets with jump prior to toss.
4. Attack consecutive short sets (two to three feet high) from center position. Each attacker receives three tosses in quick succession, giving attacker no time for a complete approach. Upon landing attacker goes up immediately for next hit. Attacker must hit a different direction each time by using a wrist and forearm snap (hitting around the block). Stress stepping back off net, opening up to tosser, and using the last steps of the approach to hit. After three attempts, attacker returns to end of line. Each player has three turns and nine total attempts.
5. Attack consecutive high sets. Coach tosses three balls, one at a time, in quick succession and fairly close to the net. Upon landing attacker goes up immediately for the next hit. After three attempts return to

the end of the line. Each player has three turns and nine attempts. Drill repeated from right, center, and left front positions, and with the coach on the opposite side of the net for overset practice. For advanced players, the coach may vary the three tosses in height and placement.

6. Attack oversets, with coach toss from opposite side of the net.
7. Attack from set. Coach tosses continually to setter who sets for the attack.
8. Attack vs. blockers standing on a bench. If blockers net on attack, a point is scored for the attackers.

MAXIM: *Teamwork is a skill you can practice; it is a coachable concept.*

Attack—Using the Block

Purpose: Hitting off the block technique.

Goal: Specific time period.

Description:

1. Individual with ball near wall holds ball against wall and then sweeps ball off to side, to both the right and left.
2. Individual on box holding the ball above net. Attacker on opposite side of net. Attacker, using last step of the approach, jumps and sweeps stationary ball off block and out of bounds. Repeat with full approach.
3. Two or three blockers near sideline (must have blockers tall enough for attackers to use block, or if necessary place blockers on bench). Tosser tosses ball close to net and toward sideline. Attacker sweeps ball off-block and out of bounds by hitting the side of the ball and following through with hand and arm facing out of bounds.

MAXIM: *Once technique is learned to a consistent/intermediate level the attack must be practiced against a block. The attacker must practice hitting around and off the blocker's hands.*

Rebound Play—Attack Into Block

Purpose: Rebound attack option.

Goal: Five rebounds off the block.

Description: Groups of four: two blockers, one attacker, and one setter. Attacker tosses ball to setter, who sets ball close to the net, trapping hitter, forcing the hitter to change tactics from attack to a soft hit. Attacker delays and hits ball softly into block as blockers are on their way down. Attacker then plays ball with a dig as it comes off blocker's hands. Five recoveries and change tasks.

MAXIM: *If you cannot avoid being blocked, remember, the harder you hit the ball into the block, the harder it comes back.*

Endurance Hitting—Getting 15

Purpose: Attack endurance, mental and physical toughness.

Individual Goal: 15 hits that will score against a tough opponent.

Description: Coach tosses high sets (right, left, or center front) to one attacker, allowing just enough time between hits for attacker to backpedal to the proper approach position. Attacker hits 15 good attacks to complete the drill; other players shag. For best utilization of time an assistant coach, manager, or team captain should simultaneously toss for a second attacker.

MAXIM: *Run some drills to exhaustion to build mental and physical strength, team cohesion, and team spirit.*

Hit the Line (Figure 3-16)

Purpose: Attack the line training.

Individual Goal: Score ten out of 15 points.

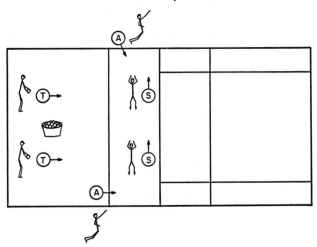

Figure 3-16

Description: One attacker left front, one attacker right front, two setters, and two tossers. Each attacker receives 15 sets. A point is scored for each ball that lands within an eight-foot area from the sideline (marked with tape or rope). No blockers. Setter for right front attacker may set forward or backset as coach indicates. Other players shag.

MAXIM: *Hard hitting does not always win volleyball matches. The attacker must choose what is the best shot at that moment for that situation.*

Attacker vs. Double Block (Figure 3-17)

Purpose: Attack practice vs. double block.

Individual Goal: Score ten out of 15 points.

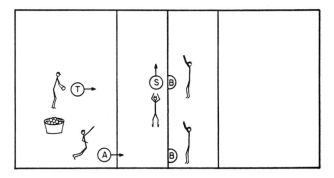

Figure 3-17

Description: One attacker, two blockers, a tosser, and a setter. Attacker hits from right, left, or center front as coach indicates. Ball is tossed to setter who sets high for the attack. Outside and center blockers must remain in their ready positions until the ball touches the setter's hands, then they release to form the double block. A point is scored for attacker for each ball hit into the court or off the blocker's hands. If the blocker commits a foul, replay the point only if the attacker is negatively affected. Attacker receives 15 sets.

MAXIM: *A short player can be as effective as a taller player by utilizing a variety of attack options.*

Attack Three, Dig, and Roll (Figure 3-18)

Purpose: Attack endurance, mental and physical toughness.

Individual Goal: The best out of 30.

Description: Three attackers in line on one side of the net, and three blockers in line on the other side. First attacker in turn hits high toss on

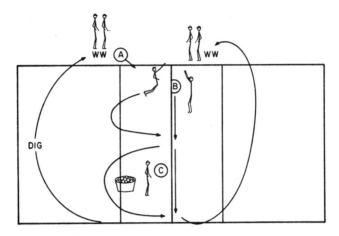

Figure 3-18

left side from coach, hits quick middle toss, hits high toss on right side, and runs back into court to dig ball thrown by coach. Return to end of attack line. One blocker blocks all three attacks and returns to end of block line. Repeat ten trips.

MAXIM: *The ultimate goal of toughness drills is hard work and second effort. Quality of performance is expected but completion of the task is the most important factor. Make the ultimate effort.*

Mass Serve Reception, Set, and Hit

Purpose: Visual and verbal communication, fun.

Team Goal: Five good hits.

Description: As many players as possible facing and holding net with both hands. Coach on opposite side of net in service position. Coach slaps ball to signal players to backpedal. Coach serves ball. One player calls for the ball to pass, one to set, and one to attack.

MAXIM: *Visual and verbal communication is vital to smooth team play. It is very important in almost every situation to call "mine" and then play the ball.*

Serve, Receive, Attack (Figure 3-19)

Purpose: Transition practice, serve, receive, attack.

Team Goal: 50 good hits.

Description: Two receivers in adjacent positions in backcourt, two attack lines (right and left front), one setter. One blocker vs. the right side

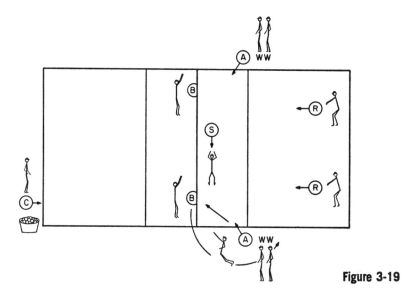

Figure 3-19

attacker, and one vs. left side attacker. Coach serves and players pass, set, and attack. After successful attack, attacker becomes blocker. Blockers shag and return to attack lines. Coach changes setter and new receivers as desired.

MAXIM: *Attacker must "open up" to the ball. The further off the net the ball is passed, the wider the approach angle.*

Consecutive Serve, Receive, Attack

Purpose: Transition practice, serve, receive, attack. Consistency and toughness.

Goal: Seven good hits in a row, or five minutes.

Description: Coach serves to two receivers who must pass, set, and attack the ball. Players must successfully attack seven consecutive balls to complete the drill. Emphasis is on selection of the proper attack option according to the set. The coach may vary the goal according to the ability of the players.

MAXIM: *A team player is one who tries to make up for a previous error by a teammate by making it easier for the next person to play the ball.*

Serve, Receive, Attack—3's (Figure 3-20)

Purpose: Transition practice, serve, receive, attack.

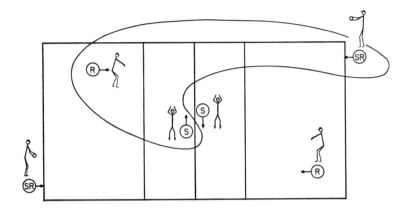

Figure 3-20

Individual Goal: Ten good hits down the line.

Description: Groups of three, one server-defender, one setter, one receiver-attacker. Server serves controlled down-the-line serve and moves into the court to play defense. Receiver passes ball to the setter who sets high to the corner of the net. Receiver approaches ball and attacks ball hard or off-speed down the line. Server-defender must make an attempt for each ball for point to be scored. After ten good down the line hits change tasks. Two groups on court perform drill concurrently. Attackers both hit from left side. Repeat drill with attackers on right side. To stress consistency, goal is to hit five consecutive down-the-line attacks before changing tasks, then four consecutive hits, then three consecutive hits to complete the drill.

MAXIM: *Never blame your setter for a poor set. A bad set is generally the result of a bad pass. Learn to make a good percentage play with any type of set you receive.*

Serve, Receive, Attack—4's (Figure 3-21)

Purpose: Transition practice, serve, receive, attack.

Individual Goal: Five good hits.

Description: Groups of four, one server-defender, one setter, two receivers. Receivers play left front and left back positions. Server serves controlled down-the-line serve and moves into the court to play defense. One receiver calls "mine" and passes to the setter who sets high to the frontcourt attacker. Attacker hits down the line and defender makes attempt to receive the ball. Backcourt receiver and setter cover the hitter. After each attack attempt, attacker and receiver exchange positions.

Figure 3-21

After five good hits attacker becomes setter, setter becomes server, server becomes receiver. Two groups on court perform drill concurrently. Repeat drill with receivers in right front and right back positions. Server serves from the right and must make a big switch to play defense for the down-the-line attack.

MAXIM: *Serve reception is a team skill and should be practiced often with two or more players.*

Server and Receiver Shuttle With Attacker (Figure 3-22)

Purpose: Serve, receive, attack training.

Team Goal: 50 good hits.

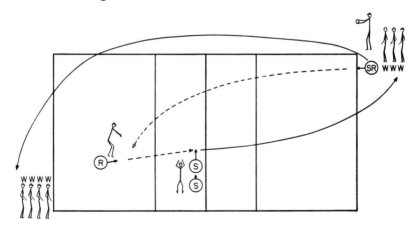

Figure 3-22

Description: Line of receivers and servers, one or two setters alternating the set task. Server serves to receiver who calls "mine" and passes the ball to the setter. Receiver then calls for a high or quick set then attacks ball, shags, and returns to end of serving line. Server rotates to receiving line. Should the server err, the server goes to end of serving line and receiver remains for next serve. If using two setters, after set move back to the ten-foot line to await next turn. Repeat drill with receivers at right and left back. Right-back receiver attacks from right front and left-back receiver attacks at left front. Repeat drill adding two backcourt receivers. Player who passes receives set. Coach changes setter as desired.

MAXIM: *The great attacker is one who is capable of attacking successfully at key moments of play.*

At Endline—Serve, Receive, Attack (Figure 3-23)

Purpose: Transition practice, serve, receive, attack.

Team Goal: 50 good hits.

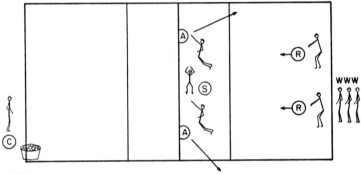

Figure 3-23

Description: Two attackers near sidelines holding net with both hands, two receivers right and left backcourt positions, one setter at net. As coach serves to receivers, attackers back off net. Receiver passes to setter, who sets for the attacker. Receivers cover attacker, attacker shags ball and is replaced by receiver who passed the ball. New receiver moves into position.

MAXIM: *The good attacker learns to hit all types of sets, best to worst.*

Progression to Winner's Game (Figure 3-24)

Purpose: Transition, serve, receive, attack, competition.

Team Goal: 15 good passes, then 15 good hits to enable group to play the winner's game.

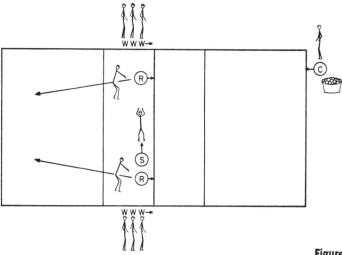

Figure 3-24

Description: Receivers touching net (two or three depending on offensive system), one stationary setter at net. Coach slaps ball to signal receivers to backpedal. Coach serves deep, and one receiver passes to the setter. Passer returns ball to coach and new receivers move into position at the net. After 15 good passes the attack is added. The setter now sets for the attack. The attacker shags the ball and returns it to the coach, and new receivers move into position at the net. After 15 good hits it's time to play the winner's game. The receiving side remains the same but three players defend the winner's side. The coach serves and the point is played out by both teams. The winning team moves to (or remains on) the winning side to defend the title. No block is allowed, and the winning side has no stationary setter.

The Block

The block is the first line of defense. The primary purpose of the block is to stop the ball and return it to the opponent's side for an immediate point or sideout. A secondary purpose is to force the opponent to attack the ball into an area of the court that you are prepared to defend. A short blocking team can be very effective if they form a well-positioned and solid block covering a consistent area. The backcourt defense is oriented according to the position of the block, covering the area outside the shadow of the block. If the block is poorly formed, the defense has more court to cover.

CHECKLIST (Figure 4-1)

1. Ready position: feet parallel, about one to two feet from net, feet shoulder distance apart, weight on the insides of feet, knees slightly bent.
2. Hands at shoulder height, elbows flexed, forearms parallel to net.
3. Just prior to jump, assume a half-squat position with back straight, explode straight up with legs, pushing off with the entire foot.
4. Hands go up and slide over top of net, penetrating over net as far as possible (attack block). Fingertips, hands, arms, and shoulders are firm and forward.
5. Hands in line with arms, fingers spread, hands positioned close together around the ball.
6. Just prior to contact, turn shoulders, arms, and hands toward the center of the opponent's court.
7. Players who are unable to penetrate over the net, place wrist near net and tilt hands back, deflecting the ball upward (soft block).
8. Hang and reach to sustain block as long as possible. You can still block on your way down.
9. Land in a ready position, similar to your starting position and in the same spot. Do not float forward or to the sides.
10. Land first, then turn head to follow play. Be ready to play the short tip, a ball hit off the block, or ball dug from the backcourt.
11. Tactics/Choice of Positioning: The single block (one-on-one block). Position yourself for a charging foul on either side of the attacker's hitting arm. Line up on attacker's approach to take away the power

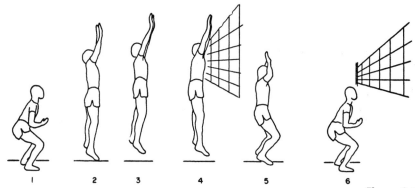

Figure 4-1

angle and most probable attack. Position hands around the side and back of ball whenever possible. Area block: Blockers take away (defend) an area of the court, for instance they take away the line or take away the angle attack. The backcourt defends the open areas. Double block: player nearest the ball establishes the position for a one-on-one block. The second blocker closes the block and then both blockers go up simultaneously.

12. Footwork: For short distances or when time is available sidestep into position; shoulders remain squared off to net. Maintain same center of gravity throughout movement. For greater distances and for quickness use crossover step (generally for center blocker). Pivot and push off, step with lead foot, cross over with other, break momentum and square off with last step (or if necessary square off in the air) and block. Focus back on attacker as you are moving upward to block (Figure 4-2).

Figure 4-2

TACTICS: SEE AND THINK, READ AND ADJUST

1. Review capabilities and tendencies of frontcourt attackers.
2. Review previous attack combinations.
3. Watch and read pass.

4. Watch and read set and analyze attack possibilities.
    A. Type of set—high or low, good or bad.
    B. Position of ball
        1. Distance from net
        2. Inside or outside antennae
        3. What does the set allow the attacker to do?
5. Watch and read attacker's body position and angle of approach.
6. Establish block position from above information.
7. Blocker jumps just after attacker jumps.
8. After jump continue to focus on attacker, ball will come into view as attacker begins armswing.

DRILLS

Wall Block

Purpose: Block training, conditioning and endurance, no ball.

Individual Goal: Three sets of 15 repetitive blocks.

Description: Stand about two feet from wall, facing wall. Do 15 consecutive blocking jumps, touching the wall with the fingers at the top of each jump. Emphasize jumping from a squat position each time, arms solid, extended, and tight.

Variations:

1. For hand movement: Reach hands and arms in different direction on each block—once right, once left, once straight up, and repeat.
2. For end blocker foot movement: two sidesteps to the right, block, two sidesteps to the left, block, and so on.
3. For center blocker foot movement: Crossover step to right, block, crossover to left, block and so on.
4. To sustain block: Jump, double touch wall while in air—center-center, right-left, and so on.
5. For maximum jumps: Jump to tape mark indicating individual's maximum jump.
6. For low squat position prior to jump: Place a chair behind blocker. Blocker touches "bottom" to edge of chair and explodes up on block from this position, lands, touches "bottom" on chair and goes up again. Feet shoulder distance apart, and generally placed outside chair legs. Blocker learns how low the initial block position needs to be and checks each time by feeling the chair.

MAXIM: *Always jump from a position of balance.*

Block and Go (Figure 4-3)

Purpose: Block and movement training along net, no ball.

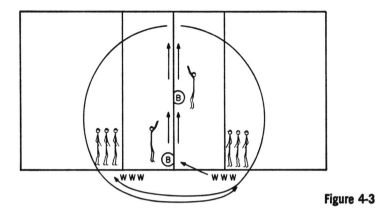

Figure 4-3

Goal: Specific number of trips across the net.

Description: One line of blockers, opposite each other, one on each side of the net. The first player in each line takes a position at the net near the sideline to block. Each player in turn blocks along the net (or several nets) and returns to the end of the opposite line. Each new player in line moves into the blocking position as the player in front completes the block on the outside and moves to the center of the court. Players may be staggered so they do not block with a partner directly opposite them. This avoids ankle injuries with beginning players. Once the technique is mastered partner blocking can be used.

Variations:

1. Block near sideline, one sidestep, block, one sidestep, block and so on.
2. Block near sideline, two sidesteps, block, two sidesteps, block, and so on.
3. Block near sideline, crossover step to center, block, crossover step to sideline, block.
4. Block near sideline, upon landing turn and look for the ball, crossover step to center, block and turn, crossover to sideline, block and turn.
5. Block near sideline, turn, imagine the ball dug by a teammate over the net, go up immediately to block a second time. Crossover to center, block, turn, and block. Crossover to sideline, block, turn, and block.
6. Give and take: Partners blocking along net left, center, and right-front positions. One player has a ball and reaches it to the top of the net while the partner jumps and reaches up to take the ball with two hands back to own side. Continuous give and.take in each position along net.

MAXIM: *Once the ball passes the block it is the blocker's responsibility to follow the ball and be prepared to receive the short tip, a ball hit off the block, or ball dug by a backcourt player.*

Block vs. Chair Attackers (Figure 4-4)

Purpose: Footwork patterns, block technique.

Goal: Specific number of trips across net.

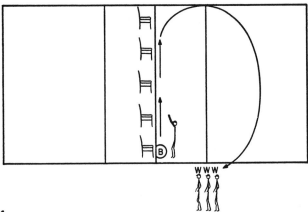

Figure 4-4

Description: Two groups: one group of chair attackers and shaggers and a second group of blockers. Five chairs are placed equal distance apart and close to net. One player stands on each chair holding a volleyball. The first blocker begins by blocking a tossed ball by the first chair attacker. Immediately the blocker lands and sidesteps to the next attacker (blocks each chair attacker). The next blocker in the line repeats this sequence. Shaggers must collect balls quickly and watch for balls rolling under the net. *Variations:* 1) Three chairs total, positioned left, center, and right front. Stress use of crossover step. 2) Three to five chairs positioned in various spots for specific attack positions at net. Player blocks the position as called out by the coach, then quickly sidesteps back to a ready position in the center of the court.

MAXIM: *Do not allow players to disrupt the rhythm of drills. Train players to shag balls quickly and efficiently.*

Mirror-Image Fake 'Em

Purpose: Block technique and movement training, no ball.

Goal: Specific number of trips across net.

Description: Two blockers positioned one on each side of the net near the sideline. One player fakes and blocks anywhere along the net and the other player must follow (mirror image) and block each time. The faker blocks about five times, as quickly as possible, attempting to leave partner in the dust. Stress proper execution of all blocks. This drill can be continued across one or several nets. All players complete drill. On the second trip across the net the roles are reversed.

Block Progression

Purpose: Block technique, timing, penetration over net.

Individual Goal: Ten good blocks.

Description: Partners positioned on opposite sides of the court, one blocker at the net, one tosser midcourt. Tosser throws ball slightly above the net to partner who attempts to block ball back. Ten good blocks and change tasks. As skill level increases 1) toss balls to right or left of blocker; 2) use two balls, tossing one immediately after another; 3) block standing hit from tosser.

Look Across and Block (Figure 4-5)

Purpose: Look at attacker, not ball.

Goal: Specific time period.

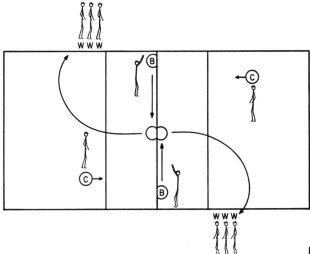

Figure 4-5

Description: Two lines of blockers positioned on opposite sides of the net. Coach or player positioned opposite each block line. First blocker takes a position to block near the sideline and looks across to the coach on the opposite side of the net. When coach opens hand, player blocks. Upon landing, player quickly moves to block in center position, but must look across net and wait for hand to open before jumping. After center block new blocker moves into a ready position and previous blocker moves to end of line.

Block and Turn—2's

Purpose: Block technique, block and turn, follow action of play.

Individual Goal: Ten playable ups.

Description: Partners on same side of net, one blocker at net, one tosser midcourt. Mock block; just prior to blocker's landing partner tosses ball to ten-foot line area. Blocker turns, finds ball, and passes back to tosser. *Variation:* Blocker and tosser are on opposite sides of net. Tosser jumps and tips ball. Blocker attempts to block ball back into court. If blocker cannot reach tipped ball, he or she lands, gets low, and tries to play ball from this position.

MAXIM: *To avoid game collisions, blocker plays those balls that can be recovered from a balanced position (no farther than one step away) without a dive or roll.*

Coach on Table—Hit Into Block

Purpose: Block technique, repetitive blocks, blockers learn to play short tip.

Individual Goal: Ten good blocks and tip recovery.

Description: One or two blockers are opposite coach who is on a table. Coach tosses ball up at medium height and players prepare to block. Coach hits ball into blocker's hands while players attempt to block ball into court. Coach may tip ball within the ten-foot line area and blockers must drop down quickly and attempt to receive ball. Ten good blocks or tip recoveries and new blockers begin drill. Emphasize penetration and turning the ball back to the center of the opponent's court. Blockers must not dive or roll to receive tip, as this could cause a collision with backcourt players.

Block-Touch Sideline (Figure 4-6)

Purpose: Block technique, crossover step training.

Goal: Ten blocks.

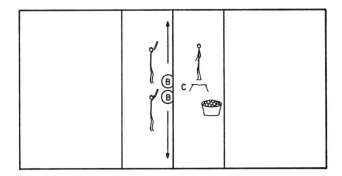

Figure 4-6

Description: Groups of two blockers. Coach on table, center front, on opposite side of the net. Blocker 1 blocks coach attack and runs to sideline, touches with foot, and immediately returns to center for next block. Meanwhile Blocker 2 blocks coach attack and moves to sideline. Continuously block, touch sideline, and block. For double-block practice players block together, touch opposite sidelines, block. Double-block players must not crowd or "bump" into one another on the block (feet of blocking partners are about 6 inches apart). Stress balance prior to the takeoff, jump straight up, do not float forward or to the sides.

MAXIM: *Practices must stress a fast game tempo.*

Bench Block—"Roofer Drill" (Figure 4-7)

Purpose: "Read" intentions of attacker.

Goal: Specific period of time.

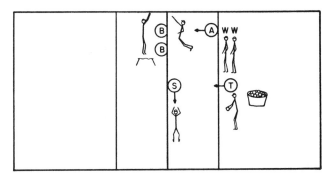

Figure 4-7

Description: Two blockers on bench, one attack line, one setter, one tosser (or coach tosses). Ball tossed to setter who sets ball to attacker. Blocker "reads" attack and moves arms in the direction of the ball.

Attacker shags ball and returns it to tosser and moves to the end of the attack line. Coach changes blockers as desired.

MAXIM: *Attackers must be aware of the block and know their attack options.*

Read the Attacker (Figure 4-8)

Purpose: Block technique, read the direction of the attack.

Goal: Competition, highest score wins.

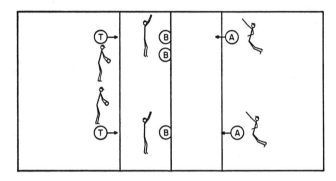

Figure 4-8

Description: Groups of three—a blocker, tosser, and attacker. Tosser overhand sets ball high to attacker, blocker must watch the attacker to predict the direction of the attack. One point is scored for each successful attack and each successful block. Attacker receives ten sets and changes tasks. Highest score at the end of round three wins. *Variation:* Add two blockers. After ten attacks blockers change tasks with attacker and tosser. This stresses teamwork of double block.

MAXIM: *Keep your eyes open; you can't block consistently if you can't see the attacker.*

Read the Setter and Attacker (Figure 4-9)

Purpose: Block technique; read direction of set and attack.

Goal: Player with most points wins.

Description: Groups of three—a blocker, setter, and attacker. Attacker tosses ball to setter who sets the ball forward or back (predetermined by setter and attacker). Blocker starts in a position directly in front of the setter and moves to the anticipated direction of the set. Attack ten balls and change tasks. One point is scored for a successful hit and two points

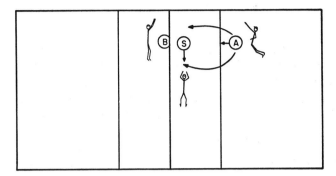

Figure 4-9

for a successful block. The player with the most points at the end of the drill wins.

MAXIM: *Always attempt to score on the serve, the attack, and the block. Always attempt to beat the opponent rather than hoping to win through opponent errors.*

Call Out Direction of Attack (Figure 4-10)

Purpose: Block technique, read direction of attack.

Individual Goal: One good block.

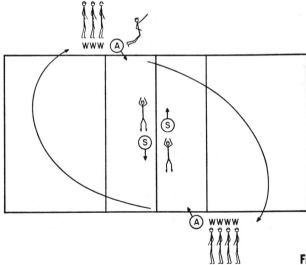

Figure 4-10

Description: Basic hitting lines with single blocker opposite each line. Blocker jumps and while in the air calls out the anticipated direction and type of attack, for example, line, angle, tip, and so on. After one successful block, blocker changes tasks with blocked attacker.

MAXIM: *Do not block against a bad set unless the attacker is very versatile.*

Attackers vs. Blockers (Figure 4-11)

Purpose: Attack and block training.

Goal: Group with highest score wins.

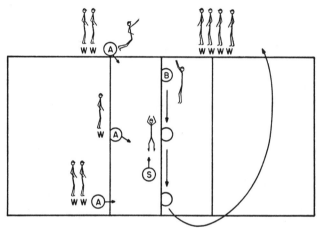

Figure 4-11

Description: Two evenly numbered groups of attackers and blockers. Each attacker in the front of the line has a ball. Left side attacker starts with toss to setter and attacks ball. Each new attacker tosses ball to setter immediately after last attack—left, center, right, respectively. The first blocker in line blocks each front court attacker—left, center, and right—and returns to end of block line. Three trips across for each blocker, and groups change tasks. One point scored for a good attack and two points scored for a good block. Group with highest score wins.

MAXIM: *Know your attackers, their abilities, and tendencies.*

Push-Block Contest 3's (Figure 4-12)

Purpose: Block technique training.

Goal: The first to five points wins. Play two out of three games.

Description: Groups of three, two blockers and one tosser. Tosser tosses ball about five feet high directly above the net. Both players block the

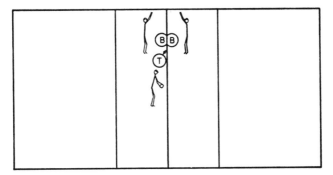

Figure 4-12

ball and attempt to push the ball to the opponent's side. Nine balls are tossed. The first player to five points wins. Play two out of three games. The winner stays, loser and tosser change tasks. It is important when the ball is set close to the net or over the net that both players block.

MAXIM: *When ball is close to the net be aggressive, "block it," "stuff it," "roof it," "push it," back to the opponent's side.*

Attack-Block Contest—3's (Figure 4-12)

Purpose: Attack and block training.

Goal: The first to five points wins, play two out of three games.

Description: Groups of three—a tosser, blocker, and attacker. Balls tossed about five feet high and one foot from net, in quick succession. Attacker has time for short approach only. Attacker attempts to hit the ball around the block primarily with a wrist and forearm snap. Blocker attempts to block ball back to opponent's side. One point is scored for a good hit and one for a good block. Nine balls tossed. The first player to five points wins the game. Play two out of three games. Winner stays; loser and tosser change tasks.

MAXIM: *Vary attack direction.*

Block, Pass, and Attack—3's (Figure 4-13)

Purpose: Transition work—block, pass, attack.

Individual Goal: Ten good hits.

Description: Groups of three—a blocker and setter on one side of the net and a tosser on the opposite side. Blocker blocks tossed ball and quickly backs off net to receive midcourt toss, then passes the ball to the setter who sets for the attack. Change tasks after ten good hits.

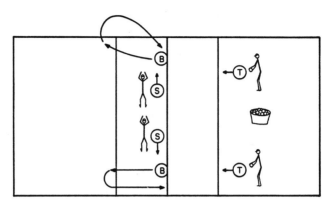

Figure 4-13

Block and Turn—3's

Purpose: Block technique, block and turn, follow action of play, play tip.

Individual Goal: Ten blocks and turns.

Description: Two players positioned for the double block; tosser positioned midcourt on the same side of the net. Mock block, just prior to blockers' landing toss ball to area of ten-foot line. Blockers land and turn and play ball back to tosser. Two blockers adds element of teamwork and decision-making as to who should play the ball. *Variations:* 1) Two blockers positioned for the double block on one side of the net with a tosser on the opposite side. The tosser jumps and tips the ball into or over the blockers' hands. Blockers must block ball or land and attempt to play the tipped ball from a standing position. 2) One blocker at net, one tosser midcourt on the same side, and one tosser on the opposite side of the net. The tosser opposite the blocker tosses the ball up for blocker to block. Immediately after the block the blocker turns into the court to receive a toss from the midcourt tosser. Stress penetration over net on the block and turning to follow the play after an unsuccessful block.

Double Block to the Whistle (Figure 4-14)

Purpose: Block technique and double-block training; no ball.

Goal: Ten trips with no errors, that is, no nets or unders.

Description: Four players positioned on same side of net—one right side blocker, one left side blocker, and two center blockers. One line of players is positioned behind each center blocker. On whistle command from coach all four blockers mock block at net. On second whistle center

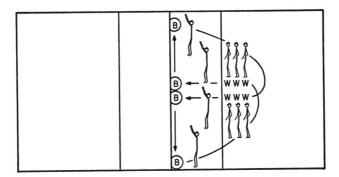

Figure 4-14

blockers, using crossover step, move to form a double block with end blockers. First players in line take center block position while previous center blockers end block. Other blockers go to the end of the opposite line. Ten trips with no nets or unders complete drill.

MAXIM: *Stress player and coach enthusiasm and spirit.*

Double Block—All Positions

Purpose: Double block and nonblock movement training, warmup, no ball.

Goal: Specific time period.

Description: One left, center, and right-side blocker in position at net, with coach midcourt on opposite side of net. Coach points in direction for formation of double block and blockers move and block in that position. Nonblocker backs off the net and moves into defensive position. Blockers then quickly return to their starting block positions. End blockers use sidesteps and center blocker uses the crossover step. Signals are: point right (double block on right side), point left (double block on left side), right arm straight up (double block in center with right side player), left arm straight up (double block in center with left side player), both arms straight up (triple block in center).

Double Block and Go (Figure 4-15)

Purpose: Block technique and double-block training.

Goal: Specific time period.

Description: One blocker positioned left, center, and right at net. Center blocker in middle, uses crossover step to double block with left side blocker. Crossover to center, block, crossover to right and double block,

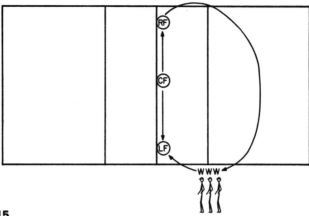

Figure 4-15

remain on right side. All players move to right, right blocker moves to end of line.

MAXIM: *Drills must be performed correctly to be of any value.*

Block vs. Attack Line and Coach (Figure 4-16)

Purpose: Block technique and double-block work.

Individual Goal: Five good blocks.

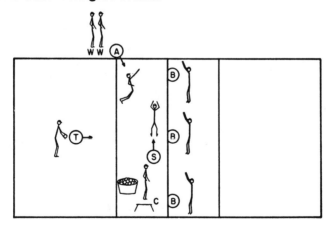

Figure 4-16

Description: A left, center, and right side blocker on one side defending against an attack line and coach hitting from table. To start drill coach calls "ready," center blocker uses crossover step to form double block with outside blocker opposite coach. Coach tosses ball and hits into the block. Immediately upon landing, center blocker sidesteps back to center position to await toss to setter. Use the crossover step to double block hitter from attack line. Change tasks after five good blocks. Coach determines blocking positions. Attackers shag ball and return ball to tosser. Tosser tosses ball to setter just as blocker nears center position. Coach can guarantee some successful blocks by hitting directly into blocker's hands.

MAXIM: Practices must encourage quick movement and quick decisions.

2 on 3 Block (Figure 4-17)

Purpose: Block technique and quickness training.

Individual Goal: Five good blocks.

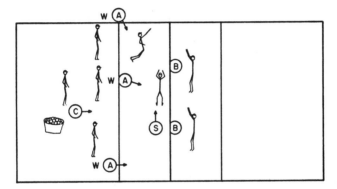

Figure 4-17

Description: Two blockers positioned toward center of court, three attack lines on opposite side. Coach tosses ball to setter, who sets an attacker. Two blockers must defend against three attackers and double block each attack. Five good blocks as a team and blockers become attackers. Two new blockers begin drill. Attackers shag ball, hand it to the coach, and return to end of an attack line.

MAXIM: Generally it is best to block crosscourt when: 1) ball is back from net, 2) opponents use short or quick sets, 3) ball is set outside antennae, 4) it is a one-on-one block situation.

Endurance Block (Figure 4-18)

Purpose: Block technique and quickness training.

Goal: Timed 30 seconds. Count number of successful blocks. Team champion acknowledged at end of drill.

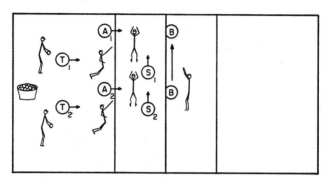

Figure 4-18

Description: Tosser 1 tosses to setter 1, attacker 1 hits at left front position. Immediately after set, tosser 2 tosses ball to setter 2 for attacker at center front position. Blocker blocks every attack. Count the number of successful blocks within the 30-second period. Change tasks. Remaining players shag until their turn. Repeat drill with attack from right and center front positions.

MAXIM: *Expect to block the ball; block as aggressively as you would attack.*

Read the Setter—3's or 4's (Figure 4-19)

Purpose: Read direction of set, quickness to outside blocker.

Goal: Timed 30 seconds.

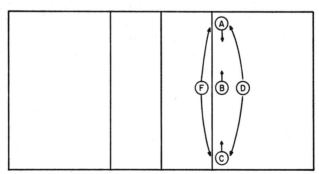

Figure 4-19

Description: Groups of four or five players. Players *A* and *C* at opposite sidelines with player *B* in middle of court. Players *D* and *F* start at either side of player *B*. *A*, *B*, and *C*, set ball high to one another. *D* and *F* must two-hand touch player with the ball. Players must anticipate, read set direction, and move quickly. Change tasks after 30 seconds.

MAXIM: *Read setter for clues of set direction. Move as ball leaves setter's hands.*

MAXIM: *Learn abilities and habits of setters.*

Toughness—Block and Attack

Purpose: Block and attack endurance, mental and physical toughness.

Individual Goal: 20 good hits.

Description: Mock block, backpedal, attack ball tossed by coach. Repeat until attacker hits 20 balls successfully. Coach tosses balls quickly giving player just enough time to backpedal and make a proper approach. On same side of the net, assistant coach or captain leads same drill concurrently. Repeat from left, center, and right attack positions. Allow players additional practice from their area of specialization.

MAXIM: *Take advantage of practice time by utilizing each player in a specific game role.*

Transition Attack and Block (Figure 4-20)

Purpose: Transition work attack to block.

Goal: Each player attacks ten balls; highest score wins.

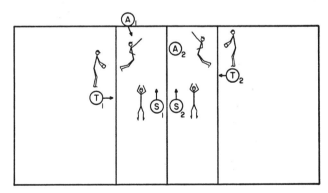

Figure 4-20

Description: Groups of six—two setters, two attackers, two tossers. Tosser 1 tosses ball to setter who sets attacker 1. Attacker 1 hits, attacker 2 blocks. Attacker 2 backs off net, tosser 2 tosses to setter, attacker 2 hits, and attacker 1 blocks. Each player attacks ten balls. The player with the highest score wins. May play off for team champion.

MAXIM: *Attacker must see block in relation to the ball and the court.*

Attack, Set, Block, Reception Series (Figure 4-21)

Purpose: Attack, set, block, reception training, warmup.

Goal: Specific time period.

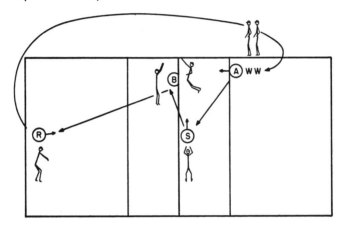

Figure 4-21

Description: One line of attackers, one setter, one blocker, one receiver. Second attacker in line tosses ball to setter who sets for the attacker. Blocker is positioned for a one-on-one block. Receiver begins center back position, reads direction of attack, and makes an attempt for each ball. After each attack rotate attacker to setter to blocker to receiver. Receiver shags ball and returns to attack line.

MAXIM: *Blocker tactic vs. taller hitter–go straight up, tilt hands back to deflect ball upward.*

Attack Lines vs. Block (Figure 4-22)

Purpose: Attack and block training.

Goal: Specific time period.

Description: Basic hitting lines with one blocker opposite each line. Second person in attack line tosses ball to setter. Attack ball and move to block attacker in opposite hitting line. Blocker remains in block position until new blocker takes position. Attackers and blockers rotate on their side of the court only.

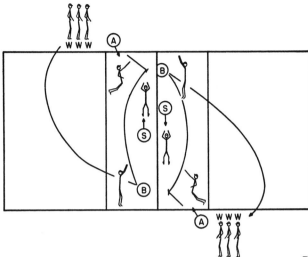

Figure 4-22

MAXIM: *Do not let the ball get between you and the net. If part of the ball is on either side, hold hands straight up and present heels to the ball.*

Double-Block—Outside Sets (Figure 4-23)

Purpose: Double-block training.

Individual Goal: Five good blocks.

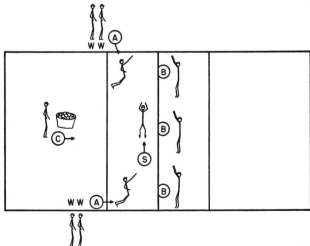

Figure 4-23

Description: Three blockers defending a right and left side hitting line. Coach tosses ball to setter, who sets forward or back for the attacker. Center blocker reads direction of set and moves quickly to form a double block with the end blocker. Nonblocker backs off net to about the ten-foot line to play the sharp crosscourt attack. After five good blocks by the blocking team a new team is selected. Stress the end blocker's setting the block early and the formation of a solid block.

MAXIM: *Always be ready to attack and always consider your options prior to the set.*

Double Block vs. Coach (Figure 4-24)

Purpose: Double-block training.

Goal: Specific time period.

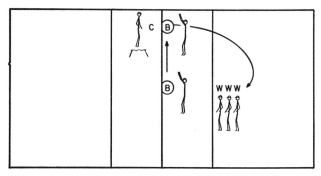

Figure 4-24

Description: Two groups—one blocking group, one shagging group. Coach on table at left front. One center blocker and one outside blocker. A line of players positioned behind the center block position. Coach slaps ball to start drill. Center blocker moves to form double block. Center blocker remains at end position to block with new center blocker. Stress good footwork, closing the block, and penetrating to the attacker's side. Repeat double block with coach hitting from center and right front positions. *Variation:* Add center back defensive player. Center back plays first for hole in block. If block is solid, center back plays balls hit deep off or over the block.

MAXIM: *Coach mental and physical toughness through hard and disciplined practices to enable players to face tough situations in the game.*

Double Block vs. Attack Line (Figure 4-25)

Purpose: Block movement and technique.

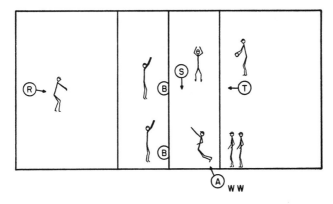

Figure 4-25

Individual Goal: Five good blocks.

Description: Attack line, tosser, and setter on one side, and on opposite side an outside and center blocker, and a center back receiver. Ball tossed to setter who sets for the attack. Double block formed on outside. If there is a hole in the block, center back must defend that area. If block is solid, center back remains deep in the shadow of the block. Attackers shag, return ball to tosser, and return to end of hitting line. After five good blocks change tasks. Repeat with attack from all frontcourt positions.

MAXIM: *Drills must provide the athlete with all possible information for the competitive game. The coach must give sufficient time for the athlete to assimilate this information both mentally and physically.*

Floor Defense

The second line of defense is the dig. Once the ball passes the block your team has a second opportunity to keep the ball in play. The power dig is the basic defensive skill and is similar in technique to the underhand pass. This skill is utilized to recover the power, off-speed, and tip attack, directly or after being deflected by the block. The extension and roll is a continuation of the dig, which is used to increase your range of effectiveness—that is, to increase the area you can cover while maintaining good ball control. The player moves quickly to the ball, extends out to dig ball with one or two hands, and the momentum of this quick movement carries the body into a roll and allows for a quick recovery back to the game. Another technique used to increase one's range is the dive. The ball is contacted while the body is "flying" in the air. After contact, the diver lowers his or her body slowly to the ground. The hands contact the floor first, followed by the chest, stomach, and legs. The body is arched, head up and knees down. The body slides forward on the follow through.

POWER DIG CHECKLIST

1. Starting ready position (Figure 5-1):
   A. Feet shoulder distance apart, weight on insides of feet, toes and knees turned in slightly.
   B. Low center of gravity with forward body lean (lower ready position than for pass). Knees in front of toes, shoulders in front of knees.
   C. Body turned into the court.
   D. Hands held comfortably out from the body, elbows bent, hands over knees, hands tight and alert for quick movement in any direction.
   E. The closer you are to the attack the greater the knee bend, and the higher the hands are held in the initial ready position. It is quicker to move the hands from shoulders to knees than the reverse.
   F. Weight equally distributed on both feet until the exact direction of the ball is determined. The ready position must allow mobility in all directions.

118

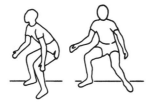

Figure 5-1

2. Tactics: See and think; read and adjust
   A. Review capabilities and tendencies of frontcourt attackers.
   B. Watch and read pass.
   C. Watch and read set.
      1. Type of set—high or low, good or bad.
      2. Position of ball
         a. Distance from net.
         b. Inside or outside antennae.
         c. What does the set allow the attacker to do?
   D. Watch and read attacker.
      1. Body position, angle of approach.
      2. Body rotation in air, shoulders and arm swing.
      3. Palm reading.
      4. Contact point.
   E. Line up with attacker belly button to belly button, shoulder to shoulder.
   F. Watch and read block position and capabilities.
3. Anticipate the attack direction and move to the correct position prior to the attack.
4. On attack contact, face point of attack and lean forward ready to move diagonally forward toward the ball.
5. Reach hands out to the ball, playing ball with two hands.
6. Dig ball up, not out. Hips move forward on contact, body leans slightly back. Curl arms and scoop ball with both hands to keep the ball on your side of the net (Figure 5-2).

Figure 5-2

7. To play high balls and/or balls to the side, turn arms and shoulders so ball is channeled into the court. Bend elbows slightly, outside shoulder higher, and weight on the outside leg (Figure 5-3).
8. Position body and arms to face setting target by dropping or raising shoulders and hips.
9. No arm swing on hard hit balls, controlled arm swing to target on soft attacks.

Figure 5-3

EXTENSION AND ROLL CHECKLIST (Figure 5-4)

1. First move is in the direction of the ball.
2. Move forward to the ball, with foot pointed to ball.
3. Lunge, stretch, and extend out to the ball.
4. Lead foot, hips, and shoulders go down to the ball and to the floor, hips lower than ball.
5. Just before knee touches ground, pivot and turn out. Do not hit knee to ground.

Figure 5-4

6. Hips must be near ground, no more than one degree angle in leg, or do not roll. Never roll if the ball is above knee. Stay on feet as long as possible.
7. Move arms at same time as last step. Drive forward to ball pushing with toes and extending out with two arms. If you cannot reach ball, put one hand down and continue to reach out and down to the ball.
8. Go straight to ball, do not pivot to get to ball.
9. Get under the ball. Turn platform to setter by dropping or raising the shoulders. Play ball near inside of knee in front of body.
10. After playing the ball, continue to extend out on side and slide digging hand out. Legs remain curled.
11. Roll to back, slap nonhitting palm on floor near hip, both arms straight and extended.
12. Roll over opposite shoulder—extend right arm and roll left.
13. Come up quickly in a track start position ready for defense.
14. If a run is necessary to reach the ball and you cannot square off, play the ball in a crossover position, then step and roll (Figure 5-5).

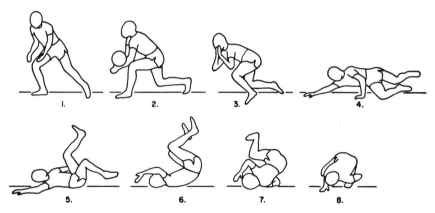

Figure 5-5

THE DIVE (Figure 5-6)

On Mat

1. Kneeling position (on both knees), fall forward with hands on the mat, in a push-up position, and lower body slowly to ground.
2. Kneeling position, fall forward with hands in push-up position, lower body to ground, pull with flat of hands and slide forward, grab floor and pull it toward chest with body arched.

Figure 5-6

3. To demonstrate good body arch, lie face down, grab feet, and arch up pulling thighs off ground, arching body and head upward.
4. To demonstrate dive motion, do pull-through push-up.
5. Kneeling position, on one knee and one foot, do modified dive maintaining slight contact with the ground with one foot, following with pull-through push-up. Land on chest, keep head up, body arched, slide forward.
6. Partners: One kneels on one knee and one foot. Kneeling player dives as above while partner lifts and pushes diver through dive by grasping one leg as diver kicks it up into the air (Figure 5-7).

Figure 5-7

7. Partners: Wheelbarrow position. Push player's feet forward and release. Diver should arch and lower body with arch and slide from chest to stomach to legs (Figure 5-8).
8. Individual dive fron kneeling position. Arch body, keep toes off mat.
9. Individual dive from kneeling position; clap hands in air before landing to simulate timing of ball contact.
10. Individual dive from kneeling position; diver scoops up stationary ball, tosses high into air, and follows through with dive (Figure 5-9).

Figure 5-8

Figure 5-9

11. Individual dive from kneeling position; partner rolls ball forward while diver scoops up ball, tosses high into air, and follows through with dive (Figure 5-10.)

Figure 5-10

12. Individual dives from ready position. Start low and stay low during entire movement. Dive forward and out but not up.
13. Individual dives from ready position pushing off both feet simultaneously for quick reaction when no time is available for steps.

On Floor

1. Repeat progressions from mat checklist items 6 through 12.
2. Individual tosses ball away and dives to play ball up before second bounce. Contact ball close to floor.
3. Partner tosses, player dives to play ball up before second bounce.

NET RETRIEVAL CHECKLIST

1. Assume a low ready position with side to net, hands below bottom of net.
2. Position yourself about one foot from net so you have adequate room to play the ball.
3. If the ball pops out of the net slowly or away from the net, contact ball with two hands and play ball back to teammates.

4. If the ball moves quickly out of the net and remains close to the net, use a fist with the hand closest to the net to play ball back to teammates.
5. Learn to read how balls will rebound off the net, depending on the tightness of the net and the speed of the ball as it goes into the net. Generally when the ball hits the bottom of the net it usually pops out and away from the net. When the ball hits the top of the net, it usually drops straight down.
6. Play the ball from a balanced position. Movement is with the hands and arms.

DRILLS

Swinging Ball on Mat (Figure 5-11)

Purpose: Strength training for upper and lower body.

Goal: Specific number of jumps, dives, or both.

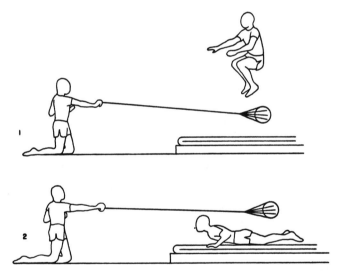

Figure 5-11

Description:

1. Tuck jumps over ball.
2. Tuck jumps over ball, lie on back, let ball go over you, tuck jump, and so on.
3. Tuck jumps over ball, lie on stomach, let ball go over you, tuck jump, and so on.

4. Dive over ball, lie on stomach, let ball go over you, dive, and so on.
5. Tuck jump facing away from direction of swinging ball, dive opposite direction over ball, tuck jump, and so on.
6. Dive over, dive over, and so on.
7. Combinations.

Defensive Shuffle

Purpose: Defense warmup, conditioning.

Goal: Timed 3–5 minutes.

Description: One left, one center, and one right back receiver on the court facing coach. Coach positioned with back to net in , center front. Players assume a defensive ready position. Coach points to right or left, forward or back, and players quickly move in that direction, keeping eyes and center of gravity level throughout the movement (use sidesteps to right and left sides). Coach also signals players to move in place with small quick steps or knees high roll, jump, and so on.

MAXIM: *One should perfect one defensive technique, either the roll or the dive, and effectively use it in the game before attempting to learn more.*

Mirror-Image Defense

Purpose: Defense warmup, conditioning.

Goal: Timed one minute.

Description: Partners face one another, one leads and one follows. Leader moves low and quick in any direction, digs, and rolls, and partner must follow. After one minute, change tasks.

Ball Out of Net

Purpose: Ball out of net training.

Individual Goal: Ten playable ups.

Description: Partners: one positioned near net, one on the ten-foot line. The deep player tosses ball into the net and player at net must recover ball. Ten playable ups and change tasks. *Variation:* Player at net mock blocks, lands, looks for the ball, and receives ball out of net. Tosser throws ball into net just after blocker lands.

MAXIM: *Attempt to play all balls before they go into the net, because it is often difficult to predict how the ball will rebound out.*

Defense Off the Wall

Purpose: Cover training, improve reflex for defense, concentration.

Goal: Specific time period.

Description: Partners: receiver about five feet from wall, facing wall. Tosser several feet behind receiver. Tosser one-hand throws ball to wall and receiver must play ball as it rebounds off wall. Receiver must be low and drive arms out to the ball. Tosser must throw ball high on wall so it rebounds moving downward toward receiver. Tosser may stand on chair for additional height. Receiver concentrates on ball rebound off wall as receiver would concentrate on ball rebound off blocker's hands for the cover.

MAXIM: *Workouts should be broken into short segments. It is less monotonous and players respond to each drill without becoming careless.*

Receive Tip (Figure 5-12)

Purpose: Receive tip with roll training.

Individual Goal: Ten playable ups.

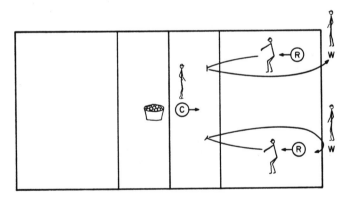

Figure 5-12

Description: Groups of four, one right and one left side receiving line behind endline. Two players in each line with coach center front. First player in line moves into court to play defense. Coach tips to each player alternately. Receiver plays tip and follows through with a roll. Return to end of own line. After ten playable ups change groups.

MAXIM: *Coach determines length of drill (goal) according to skill and execution of players.*

Defense With Sheet

Purpose: Roll training, quickness.

Individual Goal: Ten playable ups.

Description: Group of four receivers lined up in center back behind the endline. Coach center front on opposite side of the court hidden behind sheet. First player in line moves into the court to play defense. Coach tosses ball over net and receiver must run to ball, extend out to ball, and follow through with a roll. After reception attempt move to the end of the line. After ten playable ups change groups.

MAXIM: *Defensive receiver must always be concerned about where to direct the ball. The first priority is ball to target; second priority is ball on own side of net.*

Controlled Pepper

Purpose: Defense technique training, upper body attack technique.

Goal: Specific time period.

Description: Partners: one at net, one at endline. Set to partner, partner hits ball and you dig it up, they set, you hit. Continuous dig, set, and hit. Attacker hits controlled ball at medium speed aiming to the right and left sides of partner. Emphasis is on moving to the ball and playing the ball with proper technique. *Variation:* No pattern pepper. May alter dig, set, and hit pattern. Whenever ball is high enough to attack, player hits ball. Players must be ready to play defense.

MAXIM: *Make your partner work harder, then the opponent will.*

Hard Pepper

Purpose: Defense technique training vs. the hard attack.

Individual Goal: 15 playable ups.

Description: Partners: attacker at net, receiver at endline. Attacker hits while partner plays defense. Attacker hits hard but more directly than in controlled pepper drill, aiming between the knees and ankles. Occasionally the attacker may jump and hit the ball. If ball is not high enough to attack, self set, then attack.

MAXIM: *Emphasis is on making an attempt for every ball.*

One-on-One Defense at the Wall (Figure 5-13)

Purpose: Defense technique training vs. various attackers.

Goal: Timed two minutes, then rotate.

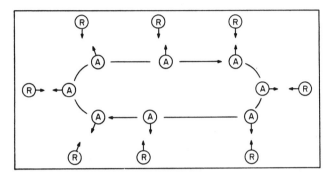

Figure 5-13

Description: Partners: receivers near wall, attackers about 20 feet away. Receivers play defense against hard or soft attack. Coach rotates attackers every two minutes. Attackers move one position to the right while the receivers remain in position. Receivers defend against new attacker. Receivers play defense three times and then attackers and receivers change positions. On the next rotation, attackers move two positions to the left. Repeat three times.

MAXIM: *Throw yourself in the direction of the ball. Put your body between the ball and the floor.*

Triangle Pepper

Purpose: Defense technique training, passing to a target.

Goal: Timed three minutes and rotate.

Description: Groups of three: attacker at net, receiver at endline, setter off to right of receiver and in front of ten-foot line. Attacker hits hard or soft to receiver, who digs ball to setter. Setter sets ball back to attacker. Continuous dig, set, attack. Stress receivers' getting behind the ball, shoulders facing setter, and setter facing direction of set. *Variation*: Receivers play specific game positions—right, center, or left back. Center back receivers pass to setter positioned in the center or off to the right of center. Left and right back receivers are positioned near the sideline and endline. Set target for right back players is to the left, and the target for right side receivers is to the right.

MAXIM: *Maximum effort must be made to direct the pass to the set target.*

3's—Run and Dig

Purpose: Defense technique training, mental and physical toughness.

Goal: Timed one minute.

Description: Groups of three: one receiver midcourt and one attacker on each sideline. Both attackers begin with a ball. The first attacker tosses or hits ball and receiver must play ball with a dig or extension and roll. Receiver quickly turns to receive ball tossed or hit by the second attacker, and so on. Attackers call out to encourage receiver to move quickly and make an attempt for every ball. Balls may be tossed or hit hard or soft in any direction. Attackers make receiver work hard to reach each attack and toss balls immediately after previous dig. Attackers must shag balls quickly to keep drill moving. Receiver does not shag.

MAXIM: *Maximum effort must be made for each ball.*

Blind Toss with Partners

Purpose: Defense technique training.

Individual Goal: Five playable ups.

Description: Partners facing same direction, tosser nearest net, receiver near ten-foot line. Tosser may not look back, but sees ball come in view as it goes over receiver's head. Receiver runs to receive ball before it bounces a second time and digs ball back to tosser. This drill stimulates movement away from the court and playing ball back to the center of court. After five playable ups change tasks.

MAXIM: *Strive to extend your reach.*

Dig and Attack (Figure 5-14)

Purpose: Defense to attack training.

Goal: Specific time period.

Description: One right or left front receiver, one tosser, coach on table on opposite side of court. The first player in line is positioned near the sideline and ten-foot line for defense against the crosscourt attack. Coach hits ball to defender who digs ball to setter and immediately

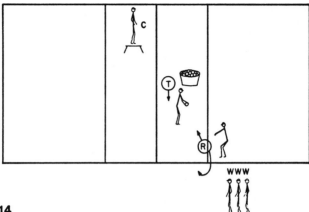

Figure 5-14

moves to an approach position and attacks tossed ball. Shag ball and return to receiving line.

MAXIM: *There is no single skill in volleyball; each movement and skill is linked to another.*

Dig, Set, Jump Set (Figure 5-15)

Purpose: Dig, set, and jump set training.

Goal: Specific time period.

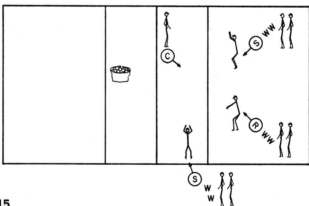

Figure 5-15

Description: Reception line, set line, jump set line. Coach hits ball to receiver, who digs ball up. Backcourt player sets to left front position, front court attacker jump sets ball back to the coach. Setter follows set and covers and goes to end of jump set line. Receiver moves to set line.

MAXIM: *Practice how you would like to play in the game.*

Dig and Set (Figure 5-16)

Purpose: Dig and set training.

Goal: Specific time period.

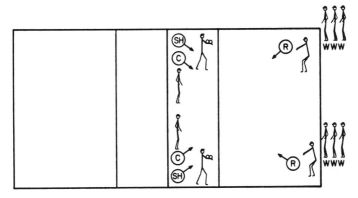

Figure 5-16

Description: A right and left back receiving lines, a coach and a shagger at right and left front corners of the net. One coach hits ball to receiver to dig while first receiver in other line sets diagonally across to corner of net. Setter follows set and remains in the front court as target. Previous target returns to receiving line. Coaches alternate hitting to right and left lines respectively. Each receiver remains for two turns, first to receive the attack from the coach and second to set ball dug by receiver in opposite line.

MAXIM: *The greater the state of defensive readiness, the greater the defensive success.*

Dig and Set—2's (Figure 5-17)

Purpose: Dig and backcourt set training.

Group Goal: Five accurate sets.

Description: Two backcourt receivers and two shaggers at the corners of the net. Coach hits from a table at center front on opposite side of the court. One receiver digs ball and second receiver sets high ball to corner

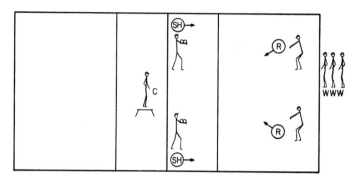

Figure 5-17

of net. Five good dig and set combinations and receivers become shaggers at net, shaggers go to end of receiving line, and two new receivers
move into the court.

MAXIM: *On a scramble play, set ball high to give attacker adequate time
to adjust.*

One "In the Pit," Dig and Set Lines (Figure 5-18)

Purpose: Dig, set attack training.

Goal: Specific time period.

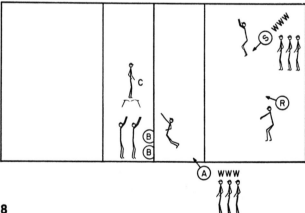

Figure 5-18

Description: One receiver, an attack line, and a set line on one side of
the net. On opposite side, coach on table and two blockers opposite
attack line. Coach hits ball to receiver, who digs ball up. First player in
set line sets ball high to left front attacker. Attacker hits, shags, and

returns to end of set line. Setter covers for the attack and returns to end of attack line. The setter must make an attempt to set every ball, no matter how impossible it seems. The attacker strives to make the proper selection of attack variations depending on the type of set and position of the block. Coach changes receiver "in the pit" as desired.

MAXIM: *Practice must provide both physical and mental preparation for competition.*

Three-Position Defense (Figure 5-19)

Purpose: Defense training for all backcourt positions.

Goal: 30 playable ups.

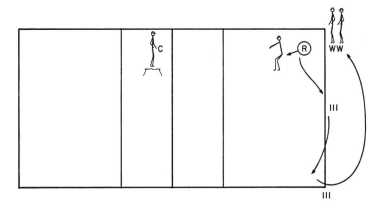

Figure 5-19

Description: Groups of three receivers, coach on table on opposite side of the net. First receiver moves into the left back defensive position to receive hit or tip from coach. After dig dash to center back position. Each player in turn receives hit or tip from coach at left back position. When all players are in center back the drill is repeated from this location. After center dig, dash to right back position. After right back dig dash to center back position, and so on. After 30 playable ups new group begins drill. It is important that when receivers dash back to their new position their eyes always focus on the opponent as in the game. The coach may hit from any position at the net. Remaining players shag.

MAXIM: *Hard practices and tough drills help build camaraderie and team spirit.*

Two-Corner Defense (Figure 5-20)

Purpose: Defense training, power and tip attack.

Group Goal: 30 playable ups.

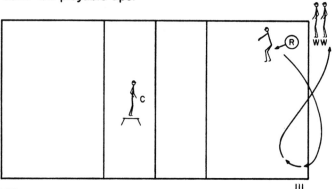

Figure 5-20

Description: Groups of three receivers, coach on table on opposite side of the net. First receiver moves into the left back defensive position to receive hard attack from coach and then receive a deep or short tip. After the second reception the receiver dashes to opposite corner. Each player in turn receives a hard attack and tip attack from coach and dashes to opposite corner. When entire group is on the right side the drill is repeated from this position. After thirty playable ups new group begins drill. Coach varies attack position. Remaining players shag. *Variation*: Coach hits two balls in a row to receivers, hard or soft.

MAXIM: *The earlier the attack direction is determined, the greater will be the defensive success.*

Figure-8 Defense (Figure 5-21)

Purpose: Center back defense training and conditioning.

Group Goal: 15 playable ups.

Description: Groups of three receivers, coach positioned center front on same side of net or on table on opposite side. Receivers positioned as diagrammed in figure eight pattern. Coach hits hard attack to receiver 1, who digs to target area. After dig, receiver moves along figure eight pattern to the left. Receiver 2 moves to center, digs, and moves to right. Receiver 3 moves to center to dig and moves left. Continuous digging in figure eight pattern. After 15 playable ups new group begins drill. Remaining players shag. Use chairs to make the figure eight pattern.

MAXIM: *Stress team as well as individual goals.*

Figure 5-21

Run and Play Ball Back Into Court (Figure 5-22)

Purpose: Center back defense training, redirect ball back into court.

Group Goal: 25 playable ups.

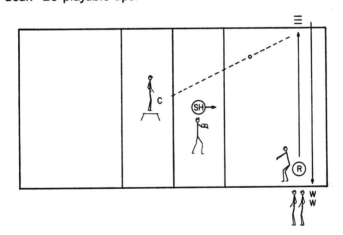

Figure 5-22

Description: Groups of three receivers, coach on table on opposite side of the net. Receivers all start left back. Coach tosses or hits ball to side of the court opposite receivers. Receiver must run to ball, extend, and roll, playing the ball high and back into the center of the court (Figure 5-5). The next two receivers follow the same procedure. When receivers are all on one side the drill is repeated in the opposite direction. Remaining players shag. Stress arms and shoulders turned to target redirecting ball into the court. Arms may be straight or bent at the elbows to curl the ball back. Do not pivot with feet to face target prior to digging ball.

MAXIM: Try hard on every shot to inspire others by your example.

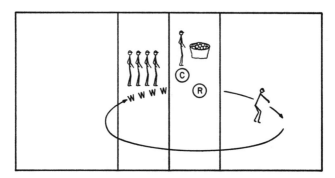

Figure 5-23

Blind Toss with Coach (Figure 5-23)

Purpose: Defense training, redirect ball back into court.

Goal: Specific time period.

Description: Coach is center front at net facing the endline. A line of receivers is center front just behind the coach. First receiver steps several feet in front of coach, looks straight ahead and awaits toss. Coach tosses ball over head of receiver, and as ball comes into view receiver must run to reach ball, play ball back into the center of the court before it bounces a second time, and follow through with a roll. Receiver shags ball and returns to the end of the receiver line. Receiver must make an attempt for every ball. Coach varies tosses short or deep, straight ahead or to the right or left side.

MAXIM: *Defense is an emotional activity. You must have a strong desire to dig the ball.*

Defense Touch the Wall

Purpose: Defense training and conditioning.

Individual Goal: Ten attempts to dig the ball. To count, receiver must "get a hand on the ball." If no attempt is made receivers' scores revert to zero.

Description: Groups of three receivers, coach on table on opposite side of the net. Receivers begin at the wall and each player in turn dashes into the right back defensive position to receive hard or soft attack from coach. After dig attempt receiver dashes back to touch wall and immediately returns to court for the next play. Ten attempts each and drill is completed. When all receivers complete drill a new group begins drill. It is important that receivers understand the positioning and responsibilities of each backcourt position. The drill is repeated from the center and left back positions. Players may practice in each position or drill in their specific game position.

MAXIM: *Be determined to get a hand on every ball. Play the ball first, then worry about landing.*

Dig-Touch Sideline (Figure 5-24)

Purpose: Individual defense training and conditioning.

Group Goal: 20 playable ups.

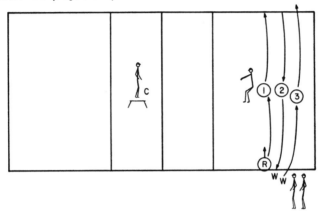

Figure 5-24

Description: Groups of three receivers, coach on table on opposite side of the net. Receivers start on left sideline midway between the net and the endline. The first receiver dashes to the center of the court to receive hard hit from coach. Immediately after dig the receiver dashes to touch right sideline, returns to center to dig, touches left sideline, returns to center to dig, dashes to right sideline. Each receiver digs three consecutive hits. Each receiver follows this procedure in turn until all players are on the opposite side of the court. Repeat drill from this side. After 20 playable ups new group begins drill. Remaining players shag. Coach varies position of attack.

MAXIM: *Encourage your teammates.*

No Block Defense—Ten-Foot Line Attack (Figure 5-25)

Purpose: Ten-foot attack training and no block defense training for backcourt.

Group Goal: 17 playable ups for the defensive team.

Description: Groups of three receivers playing backcourt defensive positions and three attack lines positioned behind the ten-foot line. Coach tosses ball deep to one attacker (in no particular sequence), and attacker hits ball hard. Receivers play first defensive play only. Attackers shag

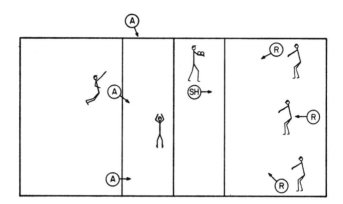

Figure 5-25

ball and return to the end of one of the attack lines. After 17 playable ups new defensive team begins drill.

MAXIM: *Defensive players must be flexible. Play an area, not a spot.*

Single Block, No Block Defense (Figure 5-26)

Purpose: Defense training—single block and no block.

Goal: Specific time period.

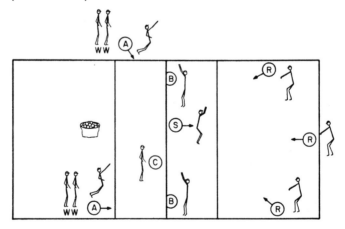

Figure 5-26

Description: Three receivers playing backcourt defensive positions, one right front and one left front attack line, one blocker opposite each attack line. Coach tosses high set about five feet from net to either attacker (in no particular sequence). Blocker blocks one on one or calls no block. All defensive players move quickly into position and play first ball up to set target. After attack, attacker becomes set target, then shags and returns to attack line. Emphasize good analysis of the attack possibilities and good movement adjusting to the attack prior to contact.

MAXIM: Stress on correction, one concept at a time.

Get and Hit Drill

Purpose: Defense to attack training.

Team Goal: Ten good hits.

Description: Groups of three receivers playing backcourt defensive positions, coach on table on opposite side of the net. Coach hits hard or soft anywhere on court. Defensive team must dig, set, and attack. Emphasize a quick transition from defense to offense and an effective attack. Only in an emergency should the ball be passed over the net. Coach varies attack position.

MAXIM: To catch opponents off guard attack off the first pass.

3's—Defense to Attacker (Figure 5-27)

Purpose: Defense to attacker training.

Goal: Specific time period.

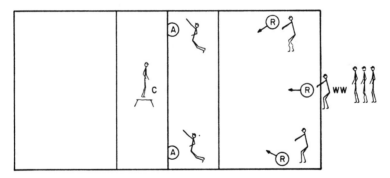

Figure 5-27

Description: Three backcourt defensive players, two outside attackers, coach on table on opposite side of the net. Attackers mock block as coach hits hard or soft anywhere on court for receivers. Receivers dig and set ball for the attack. The receiver who set the ball for the assist replaces the attacker and a new defensive player moves into position. (If no attack attempt is made, players do not rotate). Coach varies attack position.

MAXIM: Never disrupt the rhythm of a drill or neglect shagging responsibility to take a water break.

The Pit Defense

Purpose: Defense technique training, mental and physical toughness.

Goal: Two minutes.

Description: One receiver vs. the coach. Receiver positioned center back and coach is at net on same side as receiver. Coach hits hard or soft anywhere on court and receiver must make an attempt for each ball. Receiver passes ball directly back to the coach. Two minutes in the pit. If no attempt is made for the ball, 15 seconds is added to the drill.

MAXIM: *Players must experience the mental and physical rigors of the game during practice.*

Team Defense

The primary objective of the defense is to block the ball back directly or to play the ball up so a successful transition from defense to the attack can be made. Blockers and diggers must read the attack possibilities and move as a team to cover the court. Each player has a movement responsibility in relationship to the rest of the team. This responsibility involves both playing the ball and supportive movement without the ball. The key to good team defense is combining good individual defensive skills with good team defensive flow.

SELECTION OF A SYSTEM OF DEFENSE

The selection of a system of defense depends upon the blocking and digging skills of your team and the level and style of the opponent's play. The first decision that must be made is whether to defend with one or two blockers. Consideration must be given to the strength of the opponent's attackers as well as your team's blocking abilities. When players are not tall enough to block effectively it is best to utilize the one-blocker option with the remaining player covering the soft attack. In a one-blocker option, the player-back system is recommended.

When you utilize the double-block option, you have a choice of the player-up or the player-back system, or a combination of these systems. The player-back system is a "deep system," with all receivers playing deep but having responsibility for both the short and deep attack. Receivers must learn to read the tip and have good forward movement to cover the distance to reach the ball. The player-up system provides tip coverage by one "up" player while the remaining receivers have responsibility for deep coverage. It is especially advantageous for strong blocking teams that cover such a large area at the net that they force the attacker to tip or hit into a small backcourt area defended by receivers. If your block is not strong, the backcourt receivers must cover a considerably greater amount of court.

Players must understand that no defensive system is perfect. Players must be flexible, playing an area and not just a spot. Players must learn to read and anticipate the attack options according to the attacker's capabilities and tendencies, as well as the set position.

141

PLAYER-BACK SYSTEM—READING DEFENSE

Starting Defensive Positions (Figure 6-1)

Blockers stand in a ready position about one foot from the net and look across at their respective attackers. Left and right back receivers are positioned near the sideline about eight feet in front of the endline. Center back is positioned midcourt near the endline. Starting defensive positions are assumed, 1) when your team is serving with the server taking a defensive position immediately after the serve, 2) in a rally each time the ball crosses the net to the opponent's side. If players are switching to specific defensive positions, all players take a starting position so the switch can be made quickly and easily.

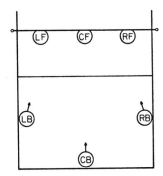

Figure 6-1

... With Two Blockers (Figure 6-2)

The double block is used to defend against the strong attack. To form the double block on the right or left side the end blocker is positioned for a one-on-one block and the center blocker moves to the end blocker. The nonblocker is positioned straddling the ten-foot line near the sideline, and is responsible for the sharp crosscourt attack and the soft tip. On an inside set (and/or when the block is positioned inside), because of the difficulty in hitting the sharp angle attack, the nonblocker may automatically release to a position under the block to cover for the tip. The backcourt player at the power angle moves up along the sideline several steps behind the frontcourt receiver (staggered positions), playing a slightly deeper power angle. Front- and backcourt receivers must be positioned off the shoulder of the center blocker, and must clearly see the attacker.

The backcourt receiver on the line directly behind the attacker has responsibility for the attack hit down the line and for the tip. If the receiver sees the attacker clearly around the block the receiver remains

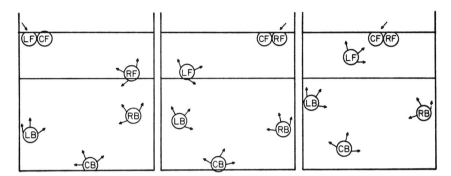

Figure 6-2

deep. If the attacker is covered by the block or when the ball is set wide outside the antennae, the receiver releases to cover the tip.

The center back receiver is positioned deep near the endline in the shadow of the block covering the deep ball over or off the top of the block. If there is a hole in the block, the center back player must move in to defend this area.

The double block for the high center attack utilizes the center blocker and either the right or left side end blocker. Which end blocker is used is determined by 1) the position of the set, that is, nearness to the right or left side, 2) directional tendencies of the attacker, and 3) preferences of coach to protect a specific area of the backcourt. The center blocker is positioned for a one-on-one block and the end blocker moves to the center blocker. The nonblocker moves behind the block to cover for the tip. The two backcourt receivers defend against the sharp angle and cutback attack, while the center back stays deep midcourt, reading the attack direction.

... With One Blocker (Figure 6-3)

A one-blocker system is utilized against an attacker who does not pose a strong hitting threat. It can be utilized effectively in the 4-2 system, in which the setter remains in the center front position and rarely attacks. It is also used by teams whose players are not tall enough to present a strong block and where the second blocker can be better used to cover the soft attack or tip.

To block the right side attack the left side blocker is positioned for a one-on-one block and lined up to block the power attack, with one hand on each side of the attacker's hitting arm. The center front player is positioned behind the block, near the ten-foot line, to cover the tip. All other positions are identical to those in the player-back system with the

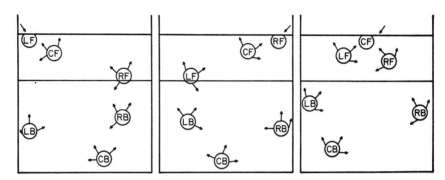

Figure 6-3

exception that backcourt players have no tip responsibility. For the center attack, center front blocks and both nonblockers cover for the tip. Backcourt positions are identical to those in the player-back system.

PLAYER-UP SYSTEM

Starting Defensive Positions (Figure 6-4)

Blockers stand about one foot from the net and look across at their respective attackers. Left and right back receivers are positioned about five feet from the sideline and eight feet forward of the endline.

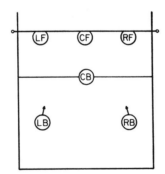

Figure 6-4

... Center Back Up (Figure 6-5)

The "up" player, (backcourt setter in the 6-2 system and center back player in the 4-2) is positioned midcourt at the ten-foot line. As the double block forms, the "up" player moves behind the block to cover the

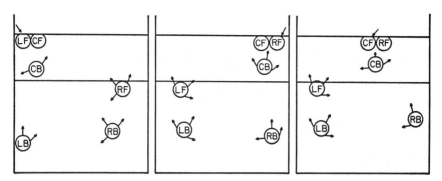

Figure 6-5

tip or short ball hit off the block. The nonblocking front row player moves behind the ten-foot line and near the sideline to defend the power angle. The two remaining backcourt players must divide the responsibility of backcourt coverage and read the attack to cover those areas most likely to be attacked.

... Nonblocker Up (Figure 6-6)

The nonblocker up variation is advantageous when the attacker cannot hit the sharp power attack inside the ten-foot line. The starting positions are identical to those of the player-back system. When the set direction is determined, the frontcourt nonblocker moves under the block to cover for the tip. Backcourt coverage is identical to that in the player-back system with the exception that backcourt receivers have limited tip responsibility. The disadvantage of this system is the difficulty it presents for the up players' transition from defense to attack.

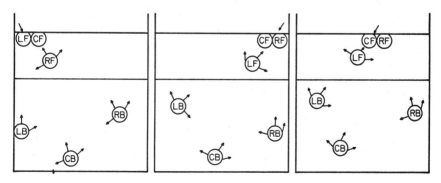

Figure 6-6

NO BLOCK/DOWN BALL (Figure 6-7)

The no block call is made when it is felt that the ball will not be hit with great speed or downward motion and can be successfully played with the dig. The call is generally made by the end blockers, as they have the most time to make this judgment. A no block is called on a weak attacker or on a poor set that does not allow a good attack. When the no block call is made, blockers quickly back off the net about five feet and assume a low forward lean-defensive position with responsibility for the soft attack and tip. Backcourt players remain in their basic defensive positions, reading and adjusting as necessary.

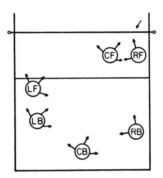

Figure 6-7

FREE BALL (Figure 6-8)

A free ball is called when the offensive team must underhand or overhand pass the ball over the net. When the free ball call is made players move quickly from their defensive position to the five player serve reception position to prepare for the attack. The free ball is very important to winning volleyball matches as it is an opportunity to score off an easy play. This not only scores points but is a psychological advantage forcing

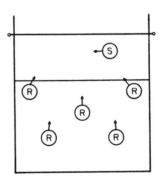

Figure 6-8

the opponent to attempt more difficult plays. When you must give a free ball to the opponent, make it as difficult as possible for them by passing the ball to a weak position on the court or to a weak passer. Occasionally it is necessary to pass it high so your team can reorganize and return to a good defensive position.

DRILLS

Defense—3's (Figure 6-9)

Purpose: Team defense training, player back system.

Group Goal: Timed or 30 playable ups. If no attempt is made for the ball, score reverts to zero.

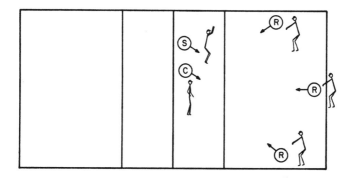

Figure 6-9

Description: Three backcourt defensive players—right, center, and left back positions, one frontcourt setter, coach right or left front. Coach hits hard or soft in rapid succession (vary speed depending on technique of player) and players attempt to dig the ball to the setter, who sets back to the coach. Coach may hit ball back to receivers, without set, when ball is passed directly to coach. If the ball does not reach the setter on the first attempt players continue to play the ball until the ball is successfully returned. Once the ball has hit the floor the coach immediately hits another ball. Each receiver may play their specific backcourt position or players may alternate positions. *Variations:* 1) Add three blockers on opposite side of net. If defense digs ball over net, blockers attack overset and defense digs ball. The coach occasionally tosses the ball over the net for blockers to hit. 2) Players may jump and attack a dug ball from behind the ten-foot line rather than passing to the setter. 3) If the first ball does not reach the setter, a backcourt player must step in and set the ball high to the corner of the net. Targets are positioned at the corners of the net to receive sets. 4) Coach vs. three backcourt receivers; no setter. Coach hits to receiver, one digs, and the other sets ball back to coach. Coach varies hitting positions—left, center, and right front during session, and receivers must look to see where they must set the dug ball.

MAXIM: Make it easy for your teammate by playing your position, by moving aggressively, and once you make a move for the ball. . . go for it!.

MAXIM: Teach technique in conjunction with court positional requirements—left back, center back, and right back receivers.

Defense—4's (Figure 6-10)

Purpose: Team defense training, player-back system.

Group Goal: Timed or 30 playable ups.

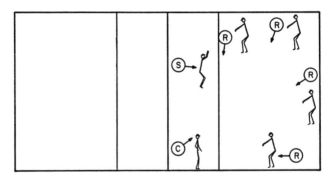

Figure 6-10

Description: Similar to 3's defense with the addition of the nonblocking front row player. Four players are now in position to receive attack. Coach hits hard or soft in rapid succession to receivers. Receiver digs ball to the frontcourt setter. Coach hits directly to players, to the sides, and in the gaps. One or two receivers make an attempt for balls in the gap using the crossing defense with one player crossing in front and one player crossing behind while making a simultaneous attempt for the ball.

MAXIM: Always be alert to play a ball deflected by a teammate and keep the ball "alive."

MAXIM: For best transfer of learning, drills must be game and court related. Practice on the court in the position in which the skill would be used in the game.

Defense—6's (Figure 6-11)

Purpose: Team defense training, player-back system.

Group Goal: Specific time period.

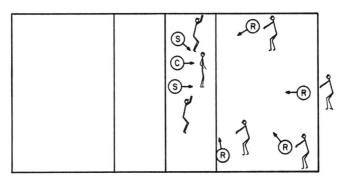

Figure 6-11

Description: Similar to 3's and 4's defense—four defensive players and two frontcourt setters. Setters are positioned on each side of the coach. In the game these two setters would be blockers. They set balls back to coach that reach the frontcourt. If dug balls do not reach the frontcourt, backcourt players must step in and set to the corners of the net. Continuous dig, set, and hit. Coach varies position of attack and may hit from right, left, or center positions. It is important for players to pivot hips to get the body behind the ball and have the shoulders and arms face the target.

MAXIM: *The coach must give players the best and the worst experience in practice to train them for the psychological task of the game.*

Defense—2's (Figure 6-12)

Purpose: Team defense training, player-up system.

Group Goal: 25 playable ups.

Description: Two backcourt receivers positioned five feet from the sideline and about eight feet from the endline. One "up" player positioned midcourt near the ten-foot line. A coach and an assistant are positioned at the right and left corners of the net. To start the drill one coach calls "ready" to signal the attack. The up player dashes to the attack area and covers for the tip (in the game this is behind the block). Backcourt receivers read the attack direction and defend the backcourt.

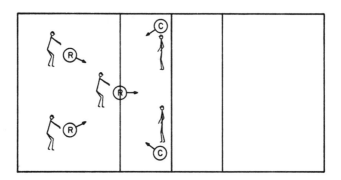

Figure 6-12

Coach may hit short or deep. If the up player does not receive the first ball, he or she immediately turns to face the backcourt receivers and sets every second ball high to the outside attacker (in this case a coach). The up player follows the set, covers, and awaits the attack by that coach. If the dug ball does not reach the frontcourt area, a backcourt receiver must step in to set. Receivers must concentrate on passing each ball to the set target. When the up player receives the tip, he or she should attempt to set the attacker on the first play.

MAXIM: *In training, never compromise; make every effort to do the impossible. Challenge yourself beyond your limits.*

Defense First (6-2) (Figure 6-13)

Purpose: Defense and set training for setter in 6-2 system.

Group Goal: Specific time period.

Figure 6-13

Description: One left front attack line, one dig/set line in right back, one tosser, and coach on table on opposite side of net. Coach hits hard or soft to backcourt setter, who digs ball to target area. Setter immediately releases to frontcourt to set ball from tosser to the left front attacker. Attacker shags and setter and attacker move to end of own lines. All players may be in set position of drill, but it is designed specifically for setters. Coach may vary position of attack and positions of attack lines— right, center, or left. This drill stresses defense for the backcourt setter, but also forces the setter to release quickly to set (overload principle).

MAXIM: *Defending the line: Move up the sideline and into the court to play balls in front of you rather than moving inside and reaching back to play the ball.*

Dig, Set, Receive Tip (Figure 6-14)

Purpose: Left and right back defense training.

Individual Goal: Five trips each.

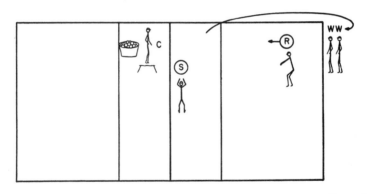

Figure 6-14

Description: Coach on table on opposite side of net (left, center or right), setter positioned in set target area near net, three backcourt receivers in a line right or left back. First receiver moves into defensive position, 1) receives hard attack from coach, dashes back to touch endline, returns to court; 2) receives tossed ball from setter and sets crosscourt for high outside attack, touches endline, returns to court; 3) receives tip and returns to end of line. This constitutes one trip. Five trips each and new group begins drill.

MAXIM: *The coach must be tough on players in practice, as the opponent will be in the game.*

MAXIM: *Mentally and physically tough practices help build confidence, concentration, and internal discipline. This discipline stops errors.*

Power Angle Dig to Attack (Figure 6-15)

Purpose: Defense to attack practice.

Individual Goal: Five good hits.

Figure 6-15

Description: Coach on table on opposite side of net attacks from left front position, left front and left back players defending the power angle. A setter is positioned at right back (6-2 system) or center front (4-2 system). Coach hits ball hard at power angle. Receiver digs ball to setter, who sets for high outside attack. Setter and left back receiver cover attacker. Left front and left back alternate positions after each attack attempt. Five good hits and a new player begins the drill. Change setters as desired. Repeat drill with right front and right back receivers. If using a 6-2 system, add a frontcourt player to set when the backcourt setter digs the ball.

MAXIM: *Setters must encourage attackers and maintain a cheerful and confident attitude.*

Attack, Block, Receive (Figure 6-16)

Purpose: Defense to attack practice.

Individual Goal: 15 good hits.

Description: Groups of six—three left front attackers, one right back setter, one center back receiver, coach on table center front, one blocker opposite coach, and two blockers opposite attack line. Coach hits to receiver directly or off blocker's hands. Receiver passes to setter who sets high to attacker. Players rotate after attack attempt from attacker to

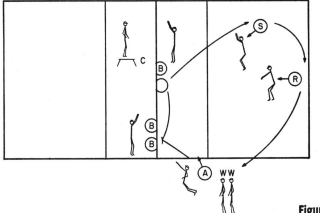

Figure 6-16

blocker to setter to receiver and back to the attack line. After 15 good hits new group begins drill. Repeat drill with right side attacker and setter in left back position.

MAXIM: *First priority on defense is to direct ball to target. Second priority is to keep ball on your side to allow transition to attack.*

Dig, Roll, Set (Figure 6-17)

Purpose: Defense to attack practice. Quick reaction on defense to controlled motion of set.

Individual Goal: Three good sets each player.

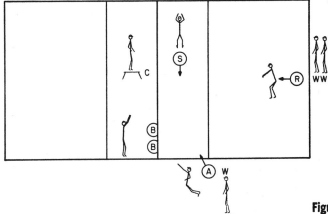

Figure 6-17

Description: Three receivers in line at center back, coach on table center front on opposite side, two right side attackers and two blockers. First receiver moves into defensive position. Coach hits first ball hard and direct to receiver who digs ball toward set target. Coach immediately hits second ball for receiver, who must extend out to reach and follow through with a roll. Third ball is tossed into air before receiver recovers from previous dig. Receiver gets up, finds ball, sets, and covers attacker. Attacker shags and returns to end of attack line. Receiver returns to end of receiver line. Three good sets each to complete drill. Stress quick recovery and a balanced set. Repeat drill with left side attackers.

MAXIM: *On difficult sets, make the percentage attack. Keep the ball in play.*

MAXIM: *Players must learn to rapidly switch from execution of one action to execution of others.*

Block and Defend the Line (Figure 6-18)

Purpose: Block and defend the line training.

Blocker Goal: Five successful blocks. Receiver's goal: 15 playable ups.

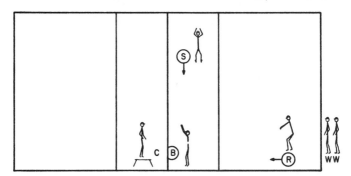

Figure 6-18

Description: One line of three left back receivers defending the line. Coach hitting down the line from table on opposite side of net, one blocker opposite coach, and one set target. First receiver moves into position to defend the line. Coach hits hard or soft into block, off blocker, or around the block. Blocker attempts to block ball directly while receiver attempts to dig ball to the set target. After five good blocks coach selects new blocker. Each receiver in turn attempts to dig ball and returns to end of reception line. After 15 playable ups new group begins drill. Repeat drill with coach hitting from left front for right back receiving line. Coach should occasionally hit the ball out of bounds to make sure players know their position on the court in relationship to the boundaries.

MAXIM: *Part of being a good player is knowing when to let the ball go out.*

Invitation to Tip (Figure 6-19)

Purpose: Recognize and anticipate the tip.

Goal: Specific time period.

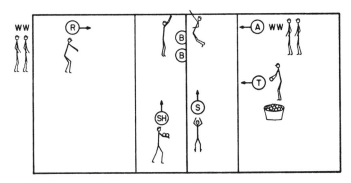

Figure 6-19

Description: One line of right side attackers, a tosser and setter on one side; on the opposite side, two blockers and a line of three left back receivers. Begin drill with toss to setter who sets ball several feet inside antennae. Block moves in to block power angle and attacker tips to outside corner. First receiver assumes backcourt defensive position, reads the tip, passes ball to set target, and returns to end of own line. Attackers return to end of their line. Repeat drill from opposite side of court.

MAXIM: *Teach players to read attack options and what they should do in each situation. By removing doubt, reactions can be made more quickly and performed with confidence.*

Tip Responsibility by Set Position (Figure 6-20)

Purpose: Defense training, player-back system. Tip responsibility by position of set.

Individual Goal: Five playable ups.

Description: Defensive team has two blockers, one nonblocking front court player, and a player defending the line. Offensive team has a tosser, a setter, and line of attackers. Ball is tossed to setter who sets high to outside attacker. Attacker must tip. Tip coverage is determined

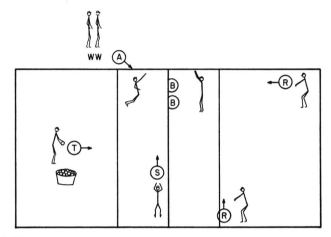

Figure 6-20

by the position of the set. If set is outside the antennae, the backcourt line player releases because there is no possibility of the attacker's hitting the line. If the set is several feet inside the antennae, the frontcourt player releases to cover the tip because it would be difficult for the attacker to hit the sharp angle. When the set is near the sideline, the defense must read the tip and then release. After five playable ups change tasks. Repeat drill with attack line on the right and on the left side.

MAXIM: *Eliminate where the ball can't go and defend the most probable areas of attack.*

MAXIM: *Challenge players mentally and physically.*

Dry-Run Defense—6's (Figure 6-21)

Purpose: Team defense position training.

Goal: Specific time period.

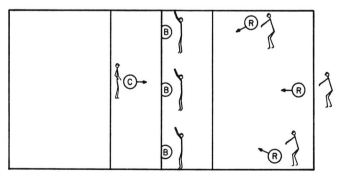

Figure 6-21

Description: Team in starting defensive positions on court and coach on opposite side of net. To begin dry run, coach calls out "ready" and players assume starting defensive ready positions. Coach points to right with right hand to signal attack from that side. Players move quickly to defensive positions. As blockers go up, backcourt receivers go low into dig position. After block, players quickly move back into ready positions and await next signal from coach. Coach points to left for left side attack. Coach holds right hand directly up for center attack with double block with right side player, or left hand up for double block with left side blocker.

MAXIM: *You must be able to model the skill without the ball before you can perform effectively with the ball.*

MAXIM: *There is movement responsibility for each player when the ball is on the opponent's side as well as when a teammate is contacting the ball.*

Team Defense vs. Coach—6's

Purpose: Transition, team defense to attack.

Team Goal: Five good hits then rotate.

Description: One team of six vs. coach on table. Coach hits ball hard or soft and team plays out point. Coach may call "no block" or "free ball" and teams play out point under new situation. Rotate after five good hits. Substitutes may rotate into specific positions or rotate in after one full team rotation. Repeat with coach at left, center, and right front positions.

MAXIM: *Play your defensive position first. Control those balls that are hit within your range–don't think so much about where the ball might go that you are unable to play the ball that comes right to you.*

Team Defense vs. Attack Line—6's (Figure 6-22)

Purpose: Transition, team defense to attack, with primary concentration on first dig and set.

Goal: Specific time period.

Description: Team defense vs. attack line. Tosser passes or bounces ball to setter who sets for the attack. Defense receives ball, sets, and passes the ball over net to tosser who immediately overhand passes ball to setter. Continuous pass, set, and attack for attack line side, and pass, set, and pass for the defensive team. Vary position of attack line—right, center, and left. Coach rotates players as desired.

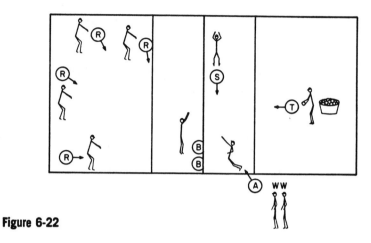

Figure 6-22

MAXIM: *Make the strong attacker hit angle. It takes longer for the ball to reach the defense and two defenders are waiting to play the ball.*

Team Defense vs. Attack Line—6's (Figure 6-23)

Purpose: Transition, team defense to attack.

Team Goal: Best defense to attack record.

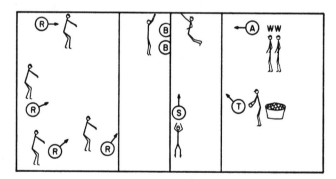

Figure 6-23

Description: One group of six players vs. attack line. Defense receives ball and plays out the point. Defensive team scores two points for a successful attack and one point for a ball passed over the net. Ten attacks for each offensive player and group changes tasks. Best defense to attack record wins. Vary position of attack line—right, center, and left.

MAXIM: *If attacker lets ball float across body, the ball probably will be hit down the line.*

MAXIM: *If ball is set beyond the antennae, the ball will be hit crosscourt.*

Team Defense vs. Attack Lines—6's (Figure 6-24)

Purpose: Transition, team defense to attack.

Goal: 20 points.

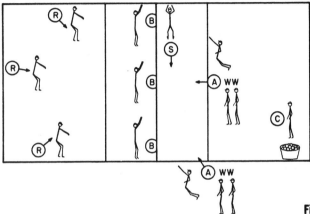

Figure 6-24

Description: Team defense vs. outside and middle attack lines. Coach tosses ball to setter who runs the offense play combinations. Blockers double block each attacker. Defensive team scores two points for a successful attack and one point for a ball passed over the net. Teams change tasks after 20 points. Coach rotates player positions on defensive team as desired.

MAXIM: *Observe and recognize the attack possibilities. Anticipate what might occur.*

MAXIM: *Contain your aggressiveness to your area of responsibility. A player out of position weakens the team's defense.*

7 Team Offense

It is the coach's responsibility to mold a team that is stronger than the sum of its parts. To accomplish this you must select a system of offense that will maximize each player's strengths. Use the following systems as a guide to help you select a system based on your team's attacking, setting, and passing abilities.

4-2 SYSTEM

The 4-2-system is the basic offensive system for beginning teams. It is effective because it is easy to understand and makes the most of simple plays by minimizing errors.

In the 4-2-system (four attackers, two setters) the two setters are placed opposite one another in the rotation so that one setter is always in the front row and one is in the back. The front row setter has primary responsibility to set. The frontcourt setter always switches to the center front position immediately after the server contacts the ball. From this position sets may be directed to the right or left side attacker. The 4-2 system relies generally on high sets and individual efforts by attackers to score points.

It is a goal of all offensive systems to create a one-on-one blocker vs. attacker situation to make it easier for the attackers to score. In the 4-2 system the setter must be deceptive so the center blocker will not know until the last moment where the set will go. In addition, the setter may pass, tip, or attack the ball over the net instead of setting, giving the opponents additional attack options to consider.

An advanced variation of the 4-2 system is the international 4-2. This system switches the setter to the right front position to set and allows for a stronger blocker to play in the center position. Attackers may use a variety of play options, attacking the ball from various positions at the net and using high or quick sets.

Serve Reception—Five Player (Figure 7-1)

Receivers are positioned in a "W" formation with the two frontcourt receivers positioned about midcourt and toward the sidelines. The left side player is about one foot from the left sideline and the right side player is midcourt about six feet from the sideline. The front court setter

160

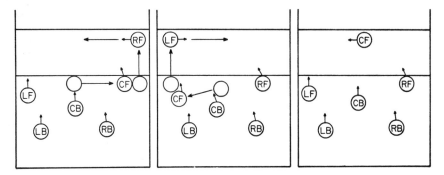

Figure 7-1

assumes a sideways position near the net facing both the server and the receiving team. When the setter is at right or left front, he or she stands at the net near the sideline and switches to the center front position immediately as the ball is contacted on the serve. When the setter is right front, the center front receiver assumes the right side receiving position. When the setter is left front, the center front receiver assumes the left side receiving position. Caution must be taken not to overlap with the corresponding player directly in front or behind you or to the sides (check overlap rule in your rule book). The right and left backcourt receivers are positioned about four feet from the endline and to the inside of the frontcourt receivers.

The center back player is forward, forming the point on the "W". Immediately as the ball is contacted on the serve, the setter moves to the setting spot and faces the left front attacker. The setter then makes a verbal call, such as "pass here," or "right here" to give the receivers an additional reminder to pass to the target. As the serve crosses the net, one receiver calls "mine" while the other players turn to face the receiver, ready to help out in case of an errant pass. Any ball that is near the line should be called "in" or "out" by the players nearest the ball. This allows the receiver to concentrate on making the perfect pass. There should be no "yours" call. This call is confusing—any verbal sound triggers players to stop because it generally indicates that someone else will play the ball. All receivers must make an attempt to get behind the serve passing the ball at the body midline. The court is small and well covered and it is generally not necessary to reach to the side to play a ball.

Covering the Hitter (Figure 7-2)

When your team attacks the ball, teammates form a cover behind the attacker to recover the ball if it is successfully blocked back by the

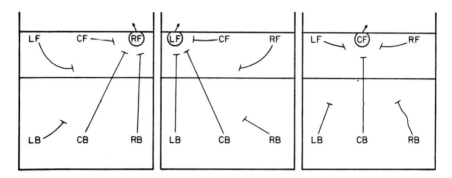

Figure 7-2

opponents to your side of the net. It is a general rule to assume that the
ball will be blocked back and to make it a habit to cover the attacker. The
setter, the center back player, and the player directly behind the attacker
form a semicircle around the attacker. This is the close cover position
about four feet from the attacker. A deep cover is formed by the nonattacking front row player, who is positioned near the ten-foot line, and the
backcourt player diagonally opposite the attacker, who covers the
backcourt. The body position for the cover is a low defensive position.
Focus on the hands of the opponent's blockers. Do not look at the attacker or the ball as it will cause a delay of motion. Drive out and forward
with the arms to meet the returned ball.

6-2 SYSTEM

The 6-2 system (six attackers, two setter/attackers) is an advanced system utilizing all players as attackers and two players specifically as setters. The two setters are placed opposite one another in the rotation so
that, as in the 4-2, one setter is in the front row and one is in the back.
Now the back row setter has primary responsibility to set and does so by
penetrating to the front row slightly off center to the right and sets three
front row attackers. The front row setter now functions as an attacker.
This system, also referred to as the multiple attack system, allows for a
greater variety of set and play combinations, creating more difficulty for
opponents to anticipate and defend. This system relies on the setter and
all front court attackers to make it easier to score.

   The 6-2 system is excellent for experienced players with advanced
skills. The setters must be able to set a variety of play combinations and
do it deceptively so the defense will not know who will attack the ball and
from what position this attack will be made. All attackers must pose a

threat, and, most fundamentally, the pass must be accurate to allow all play options to occur. As a coach you must analyze whether or not this system is geared to your team's personnel and whether it will score points for you. It must be cautioned that this system is complex, and if it is not run properly, creates the possibility for many errors.

Serve Reception—Five Player (Figure 7-3)

All frontcourt players back up to a midcourt position with center front slightly to the left of the center position and a few steps ahead of right and left front. The backcourt setter stands behind his or her corresponding front row player with the remaining two backcourt receivers splitting the backcourt territory about four feet from the endline. The "W" forma-

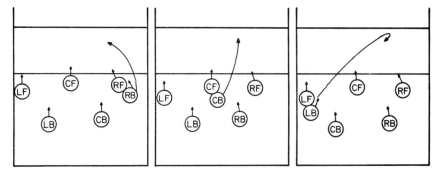

Figure 7-3

tion is formed as in the 4-2, but this time a frontcourt player forms the top of the "W." The setter releases immediately as the serve is contacted to a position near the net and to the right of the center front position. Again, it is important for the setter to provide both a visual and a verbal target for the receiver to pass to.

Serve Reception—Four Player (Figure 7-4)

In the four-player reception pattern the backcourt setter and his or her corresponding front row player move up to a position near the net. Neither player is responsible for receiving the serve. The remaining receivers form a "U," with the frontcourt players positioned about midcourt toward the right and left sidelines and the backcourt receivers splitting the backcourt area about six feet from the endline, forming the bottom of the "U." This formation allows easy transition for the setter and attackers to offense, and less confusion as to who will receive the ball.

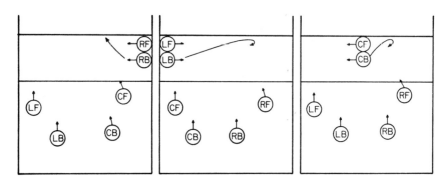

Figure 7-4

Covering the Hitter (Figure 7-5)

The cover for high sets to the right and left sides is basically the same as for the 4-2. The close cover is formed by the setter and player directly behind the attacker. The third player to fill in the close cover is now center front rather than center back as in the 4-2. This change occurs because in the 6-2, when the setter releases to set the front row attackers, there are four players in the front row and two remaining in the back. The back row players divide the court for the cover, one playing on the

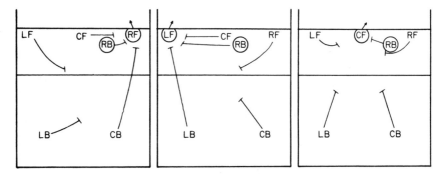

Figure 7-5

right and one playing on the left. If a quick middle attack is used the middle attacker will not have time to cover and in that case only two players form the close cover. The deep cover is again formed by the nonattacking front row player and the player diagonally opposite the attacker. To cover the middle attack all players move forward to form a semicircle around the attacker. On quick attacks it is difficult to have time to form the cover position. Players must be alert and assume a ready position wherever they are on the court.

5-1 SYSTEM

The five-one system (five attackers, one setter) is a combination of the 4-2 and 6-2 systems, with one setter who sets in every position. When the setter is in the front row the international 4-2 system is in effect, and when the setter is in the back row the 6-2 system is used. This system allows for greater consistency in that attackers have only one setter to adjust to, one player calling the plays, and one leader on the court. The setter must be an experienced player with advanced skills to successfully handle this physically and mentally demanding task. The lineup should place the best attacker to the left of the setter so this player is in the front with one rather than two other attackers, since the best attackers receive the majority of sets.

6-3 SYSTEM

In the 6-3 system (six attackers, three setters/attackers) the three setters are placed in a triangle formation in the rotation. This system has two variations—one with the front row setter option similar to the 4-2 and one with a back row setter option similar to the 6-2.

Front Row Setter Option (Figure 7-6)

Each setter/attacker sets two times and has attacker responsibility once. The setter/attacker has set responsibility when he or she rotates to center front or right front positions. When the setter rotates to the right front position, he or she switches to the center position to set. All positioning in this system is identical to the 4-2 system. Although the 4-2 system is generally accepted as the initial system for beginners, it may not be good for the ultimate development of the player. Once a player is designated as an attacker or setter only (as in 4-2) they often are unable to develop other skills. The 6-3 system with front row setter option maintains the

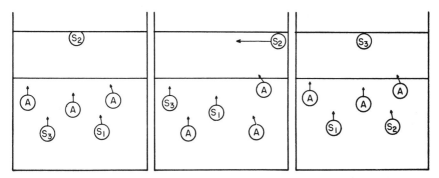

Figure 7-6

simplicity of the 4-2, yet allows all players to attack in at least one position. This allows players to develop attack as well as setting skills. It is recommended only as a progression toward more advanced systems.

Back Row Setter Option (Figure 7-7)

Each setter/attacker has primary set responsibility two times—once from the right back position and another from the center back position. This system allows for development of advanced setting techniques while allowing easy penetration from the two back row positions closest to the setting target. All positioning in this system is identical to the 6-2 system. This modification is intended for development of players as the trend for advanced play is toward fewer rather than more setters.

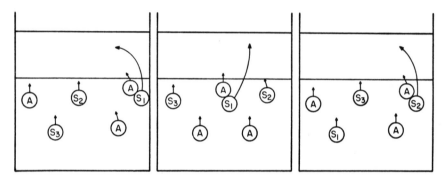

Figure 7-7

PLAYER SPECIALIZATION

Specialization is an important concept to develop once the fundamental skills are learned. It is an optional requirement for the 4-2 system but almost essential for proper execution of the 6-2 and 5-1 systems. Generally players are classified as setters and attackers. More specifically, in the frontcourt players specialize by playing right front, center front, or left front. In the backcourt players specialize by playing right back, center back, or left back. Each position has specific requirements and responsibilities.

Specialization is used to maximize team efficiency, to utilize players' strengths, and to minimize their weaknesses. Specialization is helpful psychologically as players identify with a position. Players learn their positional responsibilities and become confident in their team role. Specialization can also help the coach utilize practice time more effectively by having players practice in their specific offensive and defensive positions only. Players must know the basic responsibilities of all court positions but may spend a greater amount of time practicing in their specific game position.

Switches to a player's specialized position in the game are allowed immediately after contact is made on the serve, and this is most easily accomplished when your team is serving. When your team is receiving, backcourt switches can be made: 1) after the pass to the proper "cover" positions, or 2) after the ball has crossed the net to the opponent's side. Frontcourt players may switch positions during the pass in order to attack in various positions at the net, or can switch after the ball crosses the net. In the beginning stages of the 4-2 system the frontcourt setter switches to center front. In this position the setter sets the high set either forward or back, and it is not as critical to have the perfect pass. In the more advanced international 4-2 system a strong blocker switches to the center block position and the front court setter plays right front. This positioning strengthens the block and allows for greater offensive play options.

In the 6-2 and 5-1 systems, the team setter plays right front and right back positions. The setter must be one of the best athletes on the team, with good ball handling skills, good mobility, quickness, and speed. The setter must be reliable and consistent both mentally and physically. The setter runs the team offense.

The team's center blocker/attacker must be one of the best blockers on the team. The center blocker must have good jumping ability, quickness, and endurance. The center blocker must block the center attack and move quickly to double block with the outside attacker. The center blocker directs the defense at the net and also has center front attack responsibilities.

The center back defensive player (player back system) must be the second most mobile player on the team (the setter is the first). This must be an experienced player who is good at reading the direction of the attack. The center back player plays balls hit deep to the corners, and must cover the hole in the block.

The "up" player (player-up system) must be quick to play the short tip or ball hit off the block, and be prepared to set for the attackers.

The right and left back defensive players must be able to defend against the hard line or power-angle attack and the tip.

The right and left front end blocker/attacker blocks the sideline and center attack, defends against the sharp power angle attack, and the tip. He or she must attack on the outside or switch to another position for a play combination attack.

For identification, the volleyball court is divided into six zones or areas. The international numbering system designates these areas as

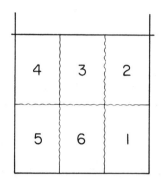

Figure 7-8

follows: 1—right back, 2—right front, 3—center front, 4—left front, 5—left back, and 6—center back (Figure 7-8).

PLAY SYSTEMS

There are two basic styles of offense. One utilizes high sets while the other utilizes a variety of low sets at different positions along the net, designed to get the ball to the attacker before the blockers can form a solid block.

High Set System

The high set is used as the primary offense in beginning volleyball, but it is frequently used by advanced teams whose style of play relies on individual power and strength. The high set is commonly used in combination with the quick attack system as a change of pace and on an inaccurate pass that does not allow the precision necessary to run the fast play. The set may be directed forward or back. It is set about ten to 15 feet above the net and should drop near the sideline allowing the attacker the option of hitting the line or the angle. The ball should be set approximately one to two feet from the net to give the attacker room to work around the block.

Quick Set System

The quick attack system (multiple offensive system) is created by the setter and attackers working together to form play combinations, attacking the ball at different positions and different heights along the net. These play combinations are based on your team's attacking strengths and are designed to beat the opponent's defense. Plays may be preassigned and called by the setter or attacker prior to your team's being on offense, or may be situational, and called by the attacker during the pass to the setter. Each set or series of sets is indicated with a letter or number and is called verbally or by use of hand signs.

SET LANGUAGE (Figure 7-9)

Slow Outside Shoot (4)

Ball set approximately four to six feet above the net and one to two feet back from the net. The arch of the ball should land about three feet outside the sideline, giving the attacker the option to hit the line or the angle shot. This medium fast looping set is effective because it does not require the precision of the fast set, while at the same time does not give the block sufficient time to form a solid block.

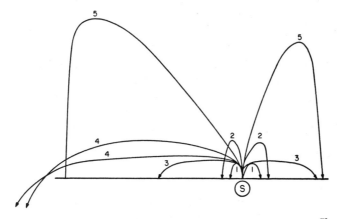

Figure 7-9

Quick Outside Shoot (4)

Ball set low and quick along the net, about two to three feet above the net, and one to two feet back from net. The set is quick with less arch making it very difficult for the center blocker to close the block. The attacker jumps just after the ball leaves setter's hands.

Inside Front Shoot (3)

Ball set quick and low along the net three to five feet from the setter and set to the height of the attacker's reach. Similar timing to the quick front set with attacker jumping just prior to set.

Back Shoot (3)

Ball backset low and quick about three to five feet behind the setter and set to the height of the attacker's reach. Similar timing to the quick front set with attacker jumping prior to set.

Quick Front Set (1)

Ball set one to two feet in front of the setter and moving toward the net. The attacker jumps prior to the set and ball is set to the height of the attacker's reach. The setter determines the timing and often the direction of the attack.

Quick Backset (1)

Similar to the front set with the attacker jumping behind the setter prior to the set.

Medium High Set (2)

Ball set about two to four feet above the net in a loopy fashion. Ball may be directed forward or back. This set may be used alone or in combination with the quick front or backsets to form the tandem play.

Tandem Time Differential (2)

The purpose of the tandem is to move two attackers toward one blocker (overload), the first attacker going in for the quick 1 or 3 set, followed closely by the second attacker ready to hit a slightly higher set to the side or behind the first attacker. The setter must feel and see the blocker and if the blocker does not jump with the first attacker, the setter should set immediately. If the blocker goes up with the first attacker, the setter sets the second attacker before the blocker can recover. The quick 1 or 3 set must pose a threat for the tandem to be effective. The tandem may be run straight or with two players crossing in an "X" formation.

High Set (5)

Ball set ten to 15 feet above the net dropping near the sideline, one to two feet back from the net.

DRILLS

Offense Systems Coach Toss (Figure 7-10)

Purpose: Offense system practice.

Goal: Specific time period or specific number of successful attacks or play combinations.

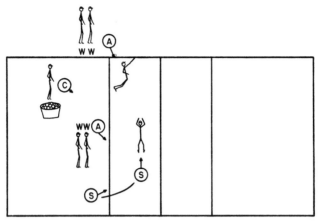

Figure 7-10

Description: One, two, or three attack lines, two setters alternating set task. Coach tosses ball to setter who runs the offense. Attackers practice various types of sets and play combinations. The coach challenges the setter by tossing to various spots on the court to accustom the setter to all types of passes in the game. Attackers hit, shag, and return to the end of an attack line. For 6-2 system practice with a penetrating setter the coach tosses ball to setter, who releases from the right back position behind the ten-foot line. After set and cover, setter returns to right back position at the ten-foot line area and second setter releases for next toss. Setters alternate, releasing from the right, center, and left back positions. Drill should be practiced against the block as quickly as proficiency allows. *Variation*: Add receiver center back on same side as attackers, with coach on opposite side of net. Coach tosses to receiver who passes to the setter (Figure 7-11).

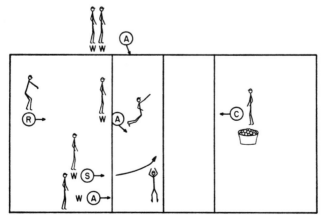

Figure 7-11

MAXIM: *Although all players must learn and practice all front- and backcourt positions, players should spend the majority of time practicing in their specific game role.*

MAXIM: *Percentages favor hitting the ball into the moving blocker.*

Individual Free Ball to Attacker With Pass (Figure 7-12)

Purpose: Transition, free ball to attack.

Group Goal: Convert 70 percent of attacks successfully, that is, seven out of ten.

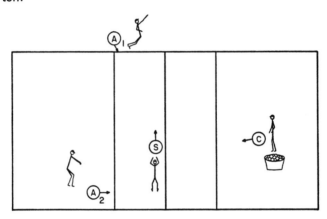

Figure 7-12

Description: Groups of three—one left and one right front attacker and one setter positioned center front. Coach on opposite side of net. Coach tosses ball to either attacker, who passes to the setter. Setter may set either attacker. Immediately after attacker lands, the coach tosses the next free ball for the attackers to pass. Continuous pass, set, and attack. Coach tosses a total of ten balls for the attackers. Attackers count the number of good attacks as a team.

Individual Free Ball to Attacker With Pass (Figure 7-13)

Purpose: Transition: free ball to attack.

Group Goal: Convert 70 percent of attacks successfully.

Description: Groups of five, two groups performing drill simultaneously. Each group has two attackers, one setter, one blocker, and one tosser. Tosser throws ball over net to a position behind the ten-foot line. Attacker

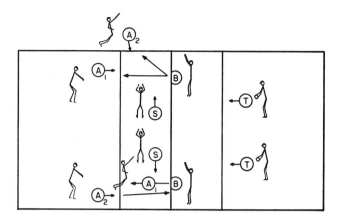

Figure 7-13

1 overhand passes ball to setter and attacker 2 hits. Attacker 2 immediately backpedals and receives toss, overhand passes to setter, and attacker 1 hits. Continuous pass and attack. Each attacker hits ten times and changes tasks. Attackers may hit high or quick sets.

MAXIM: *A free ball is a gift. One must have a perfect pass and score at least 70 percent of the time.*

Offense Systems Coach Toss—Repetitive (Figure 7-14)

Purpose: Offense system practice.

Goal: Specific number of tosses or successful attacks.

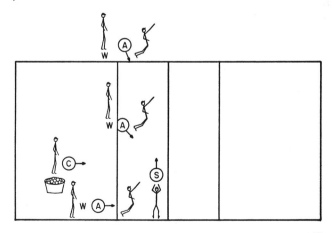

Figure 7-14

Description: Two groups of three attackers positioned left, center, and right front, and one setter. Coach tosses to setter who runs system designated by coach. After each attack attackers backpedal quickly to prepare for next play, and attacker (player who just attacked ball) exchanges position with second player in line. Players in drill do not shag. Coach tosses balls rapidly to the setter giving attackers just enough time to sufficiently prepare for the attack.

MAXIM: *Hit the ball off the block when the set is near the sideline and close to the net.*

Team Free Ball to Attacker—Attackers Pass (Figure 7-15)

Purpose: Transition: free ball to attack.

Goal: Convert 70 percent of attacks.

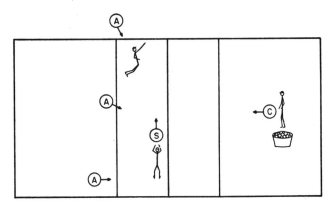

Figure 7-15

Description: Groups of three attackers (6-2) or two attackers (4-2), one setter. Coach on opposite side of the net tosses ball midcourt for attackers who overhand pass to the setter. Attackers approach and setter sets play combinations. After attack, backpedal quickly to receive next toss. Continuous attack, backpedal, pass and attack. After seven successful attacks a new group begins drill. It is important that attackers move off net quickly to pass the free ball and that each attacker call out the type of set preferred. Even when plays are prearranged it is helpful to the setter to hear where the attacker is positioned and that they are ready to attack. *Variation:* (Figure 7-16). Second group of attackers added. After attack, attackers backpedal and receive next toss from coach while second group of attackers approach for the hit. Attacker groups change positions after each attack. Continuous attack, backpedal, pass, and attack, with previous attackers backing up to pass each new free ball. Fifteen successful attacks to complete drill.

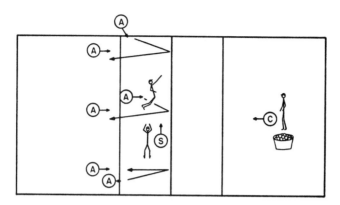

Figure 7-16

MAXIM: *Talk it up with teammates; show appreciation, compliment one another, attacker acknowledges setter, setter acknowledges passer.*

MAXIM: *Systems and tactics must be broken down into parts and taught in a progression similar to that of the skill techniques. All these drill parts are then pieced together to form the full game.*

Rapid Hitting With Rapid Fire Set (Figure 7-17)

Purpose: Repetitive setting and attack practice.

Individual Goal: Count the number of good hits out of ten.

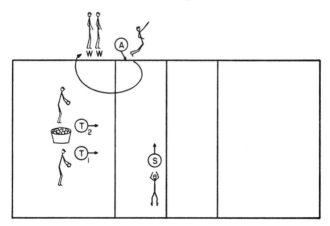

Figure 7-17

Description: Two tossers, one setter, and three attackers. Tosser 1 tosses to setter who sets first attacker. Tosser 2 tosses ball immediately after first attacker lands. After each hit, attackers move to the right and to the end of the line. After ten hits each new group begins drill. Repeat drill with attack line at right, center, and left positions. May use various types of sets—high sets, quick sets, forward, or back.

MAXIM: *First priority in attack is good contact, placement, and control, then add speed and power.*

Attack Twice With Rapid Fire Set (Figure 7-18)

Purpose: Repetitive setting, attack practice for play sets.

Team Goal: Specific time period.

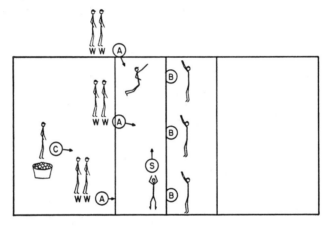

Figure 7-18

Description: One blocker opposite each of three attack lines, and one setter. Coach tosses to setter who sets attacker. Coach tosses next ball immediately after attacker lands. Setter sets same attacker. Each attacker hits twice in succession. Attacker must attack second ball with shortened approach. After hit, attacker replaces blocker on opposite side. Blocker shags and goes to end of an attack line. Setter sets two balls to left line, center line, and right line and starts series again. Coach changes setters as desired. Types of sets designated by coach.

MAXIM: *After each attack, analyze its effectiveness–this was effective. . . next time I should. . . it might be better to. . ..*

Rapid Fire—Two Setters (Figure 7-19)

Purpose: Set and attack training and conditioning.

Individual Goal: Count the number of good hits out of ten.

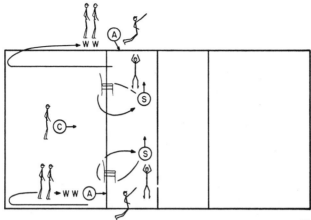

Figure 7-19

Description: Three attackers in right line and three attackers in left line, two setters, two chairs. Coach alternates tosses to setters. After each set the setter moves in direction of set, around chair, and quickly back to the original set position. Attacker hits, runs to touch endline, and returns to own line. Left side setter sets forward and right side setter backsets. Change setter as desired. After ten hits each new group begins. Players attack on both the right and left sides.

MAXIM: *Stress teamwork in the game, in practice, in drills, and in shagging.*

Serve Reception and Attack (Figure 7-20)

Purpose: Set practice off serve reception, system practice.

Goal: Specific time period.

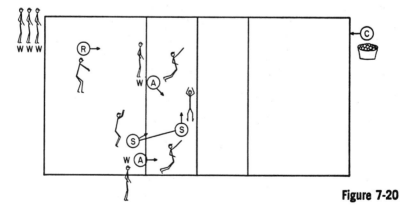

Figure 7-20

Description: Receiver line, one or two attack lines, two setters alternate the set task. Coach serves ball to first player in receiver line. Offense runs attack patterns. Coach serves immediately after attacker lands. Attacker shags and goes to end of attack line and receivers go to the end of receiver line. Coach rotates groups as desired. Start with one attack line and then add two for various play combinations. Later add blockers. For beginners, a toss from the coach in place of the serve may be used as a progression leading up to the serve.

MAXIM: *Attackers should call out the play name, number, or letter 1) as a reminder for the setter, 2) to ready attacker for the play, and 3) to hold the attention of the blocker.*

Serve Reception With Attack—Rapid Fire Set (Figure 7-21)

Purpose: Serve reception, attack and set training.

Group Goal: 15 good hits.

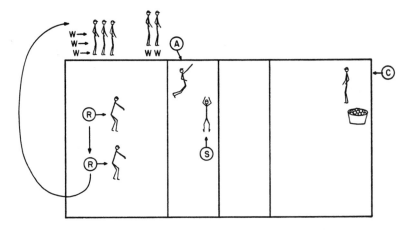

Figure 7-21

Description: Line of receivers, line of attackers, and a setter. Coach serves one ball immediately after another. First receiver passes ball from the left back and then the right back position, and returns to end of receiver line. Setter must move quickly to set each ball. First attacker hits ball, shags, and returns to end of attack line. After 15 good hits attackers and receivers change tasks. Add blockers.

MAXIM: *Vary direction and type of attack.*

Attack Systems Off Serve Receive (Figure 7-22)

Purpose: Offense system practice off serve reception.

Goal: Rotate on three attack errors.

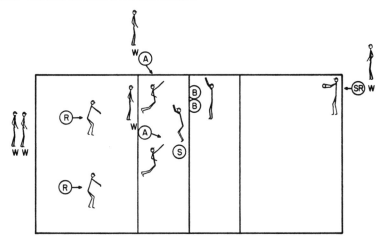

Figure 7-22

Description: Four groups: servers, receivers, blockers, and attackers, and a stationary setter. Two receivers share backcourt passing responsibilities. After each pass attempt new receiver moves onto court. Attackers are positioned center front and right or left front. Serve, pass, set, and attack. After attack, new attacker rotates into position. Players rotate within own groups. After three attack errors groups rotate receivers to attackers to blockers to servers to receivers.

Situational Serve Reception—Setter Left Back (Figure 7-23)

Purpose: Serve, receive, attack training; 6-2 system with setter penetrating from left back position.

Goal: Specific time period.

Description: Left back receiver, 'center front and left front receiver/attackers, left back setter, two blockers, and a server. Server serves primarily down the line to the left back position. Setter moves quickly to the set position and sets play combinations to left and center front attackers. Utilize players in their specific game positions and in the proper game rotation.

MAXIM: *Break the game into parts and practice them separately.*

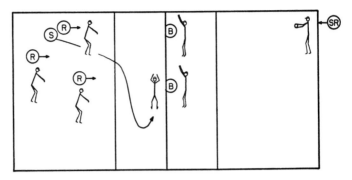

Figure 7-23

MAXIM: *When frontcourt player passes the ball, think pass first, then think attack.*

Situational Serve Reception—Setter Right Back (Figure 7-24)

Purpose: Serve, receive, attack training; 6-2 or 4-2 system.

Goal: Specific time period.

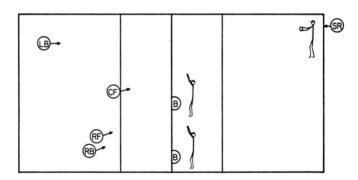

Figure 7-24

Description: 6-2 system: Left back receiver, center front and right front attackers, right back setter, two blockers, and a server. Serve is directed toward left back receiver. Setter moves quickly to the set position to set play combinations to right and center front attackers. Utilize players in their specific game positions and in the proper game rotation. 4-2 system: Left back receiver, right and left front attacker, setter center front.

MAXIM: *Drills must re-create game situations as closely as possible so players gain confidence through success in practice.*

MAXIM: *Groups of players should practice together according to the way they will play in the game.*

Read the Defense (Figure 7-25)

Purpose: Practice "reading the defense." Place the tip or attack oppo-site the defensive player.

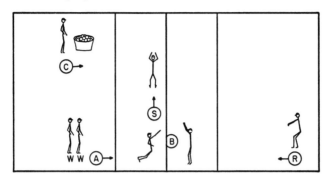

Figure 7-25

Goal: Specific time period.

Description: Attack line, one blocker, one receiver, one setter. Coach tosses to setter who sets attacker. Attacker looks just before set is made to see if receiver is up or back. If back, tip, and if up, hit deep down the line. Attacker attempts to beat defense.

MAXIM: *Teach players to make the proper tactical decision in each situation they will face in the game. Once in the game the correct response is automatic.*

1 vs. 1

Purpose: Warmup, 1 vs. 1 competition.

Individual Goal: Win.

Description: Divide court into three equal sections, mark with tape or chalk, and use antennae (optional). 1 vs. 1 games in each section. Begin game with the serve. May contact the ball one, two, or three times before sending it over the net. May use pass, set, and jump sets only. The first player to 15 and ahead by two wins the game. Players must concentrate on out-thinking the opponent with well-placed shots.

MAXIM: *Practices must have achievable objectives.*

2 vs. 2

Purpose: Warmup, 2 vs. 2 competition.

Team Goal: Win.

Description: Divide court into two equal sections, mark with tape or chalk, and use antennae (optional). 2 vs. 2 games in each section.

Regulation volleyball rules are used. The first team to 15 points and ahead by two points wins. Drill may be repeated playing competition with opponents diagonally across from one another with all crosscourt play.

MAXIM: *Do not allow a teammate to take the blame for your mistake.*

3 vs. 3—Roving Setter (Figure 7-26)

Purpose: Warmup, 3 vs. 3 competition, setter movement.

Team Goal: Win.

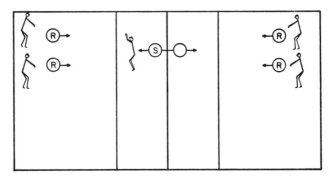

Figure 7-26

Description: Divide court into two equal sections, mark with tape or chalk, and use antennae (optional). 3 vs. 3 games in each section with a roving setter who switches under the net to set every second ball (total of five players on each half of court). The first team to 15 points and ahead by two wins. The setter always wins.

MAXIM: *Players should not correct teammates' errors unless they ask for help. This is the coach's job.*

Mini-Volleyball 3 vs. 3

Purpose: 3 vs. 3 competition.

Team Goal: Win.

Description: Divide court into two equal sections, mark with tape or chalk, and use antennae (optional). 3 vs. 3 competition with all regulation volleyball rules in effect. The first team to 15 points and ahead by two wins.

MAXIM: *Leave each practice a little better than when you came in.*

3 vs. 3 Dig, Set, Attack, Rotate (Figure 7-27)

Purpose: Transition practice, consistency, and control.

Team Goal: Specific time period, high number of consecutive plays over the net in one rally.

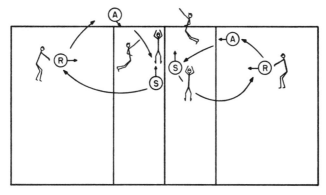

Figure 7-27

Description: Divide court into two equal sections, mark with tape or chalk, and use antennae (optional). 3 vs. 3 games in each section. Players on each side are classified as receiver, setter, and attacker. Drill begins with overhand pass to opponents. Receiver passes to setter who sets for the attack. Attacker hits controlled attack to opponent receiver. Immediately after the attack, players on that side rotate attacker to setter, setter to receiver, and receiver to attacker. Continuous pass, set, controlled attack, and rotation. Strive to increase the number of times the ball can be played over the net in one rally. Alternate sides for the initial overhand pass. For beginners' progression, begin with free ball pass or jump pass in place of the attack.

MAXIM: *Drills must be repeated until proficiency is acquired.*

Controlled Rally Attack, Reception, and Set Lines (Figure 7-28)

Purpose: Transition practice, consistency, and control.

Group Goal: Specific time period. High number of consecutive plays over the net in one rally.

Description: Two groups: one group on each side of the net. Minimum of six in a group. Groups subdivided into two left side attackers, two right side setters, and two left back receivers. Begin rally with an overhand pass to opponent's receiving line. Receiver digs ball, setter sets, attacker hits controlled shot to opponent receiver. Players rotate after each attack on their side only. Attacker to end of set line, setter to reception line, and Keep the ball in play. For beginners' progression, begin with free ball pass or jump pass in place of the attack.

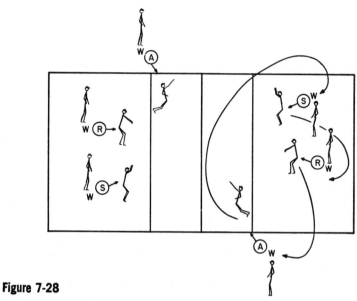

Figure 7-28

MAXIM: *You are responsible for yourself: to train, to work hard in practice and in the game.*

Controlled Rally—3 Receivers (Figure 7-29)

Purpose: Transition practice, controlled rally.

Group Goal: Five balls over the net in one rally, then rotate. Both teams rotate back to original position to complete drill.

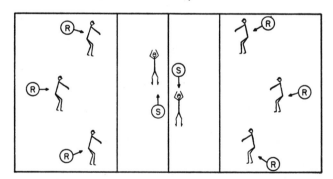

Figure 7-29

Description: Two groups of four—three backcourt players and one frontcourt setter/blocker on each side of the net. Begin rally with an overhand pass to opponents. The goal is a continuous, controlled pass, set, and attack rally. For advanced players attack from behind the ten-foot line. The frontcourt player sets and is the only player who may block. After five or more balls over net in continuous rally both sides rotate. When both teams rotate back to original position the drill is complete. Do not stop rally at five, but continue the rally as long as possible.

MAXIM: Stress positive visual communications on the court–positive postures and gestures.

Controlled Frontcourt Rally (Figure 7-30)

Purpose: Frontcourt transition practice, no block call.

Group Goal: Specific time period or ten balls over net in one rally.

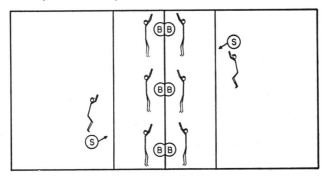

Figure 7-30

Description: For 6-2 system: Three front row players and a back row setter on each side of the net. Setter begins drill with overhand pass to opponents. Attackers back off net to overhand pass, set, and prepare to attack. Defense is positioned to block, but just prior to the attack, blockers call "no block," backpedal, and receive overhand jump set or tip from attacker. Continuous pass, set, jump set, or tip to opponents near ten-foot line. For 4-2-system: Use three frontcourt players with setter in the center front position.

MAXIM: Utilize the tip on good sets–do not use it only in an emergency.

MAXIM: Tip because it's a smart play and not because you are afraid to hit.

Invisible Ball Drill

Purpose: Mental and physical rehearsal of the game, conditioning.

Individual Goal: Two minutes in a specific frontcourt position and two minutes in a specific backcourt position.

Description: Maximum of three players on each side of the court, two frontcourt and one backcourt players, or vice-versa. Players are instructed to play a specific backcourt or frontcourt position—right, left, or center. Players must visualize all possible situations that could potentially occur in the game while in that position. Players then enact those situations. Skills should be modeled mechanically perfectly. (If necessary, do skills at ¾ speed and progress to full speed.) Players communicate as they would in the game—"got it," "mine," "cover," and so on. Players work completely independently of one another. Continue volleyball movement for two minutes and change positions.

MAXIM: *Stress mental and physical skills. Integrate techniques and tactics to form a thinking player.*

Dry-Run Team Serve Receive to Attack—6's

Purpose: Model movement patterns for pass, set, attack, and cover.

Goal: Specific time period.

Description: Team begins in serve reception positions, coach on opposite side of net, facing team. Coach calls out command and players respond verbally and with movement. Coach calls out ready: players respond with "ready position" and prepare to receive the serve. Coach calls out service: receivers call out "pass" and model movement while setter calls "mine" and is ready to set the ball. Coach points to left, right, or center for the attack while players respond with a mock attack to that side and call out "cover." As attacker goes up to hit, remaining players go low to cover. *Variation:* Add movement for entire point. After coverage coach calls out defense: players respond with defense and move to starting defensive positions. Coach points to left, right, or center and defense defends attack. As blockers go up to block, receivers go low on defense to play ball. Continue for several attacks and then repeat from serve reception positions. Coach may say "defense," and immediately after players respond by calling out "defense," coach claps three times and by the third clap all players must be in the proper position.

MAXIM: *Develop movement patterns and linking actions so they become automatic in the game.*

Servers vs. Team Serve Receivers—6's

Purpose: Team serve, receive, attack training.

Goal: Receivers rotate back to original positions.

Description: Receiving team positioned to receive serve. Servers on opposite side of court. Servers alternate serving after each play. Server must serve five tough serves that cannot be converted to an attack in order to rotate into the receiving lineup (coach designates the position to be played). After three good attacks the receiving team rotates. For more advanced teams, rotate on three consecutive good plays.

MAXIM: *Drills must copy things that happen in the game.*

Three-Minute Team Serve Reception—6's

Purpose: Repetitive team serve reception training.

Team Goal: As many good passes to the setter as possible within three minutes. Strive to beat previous records.

Description: One six-player team on one side and one server on the other. Server serves and receiver passes to setter. Setter sets ball and attacker jump sets ball back to the server (or catches ball and throws it back to the server). Server varies direction of serve and serves as many balls as possible in the three-minute time period. Only one ball is used. The setter must set every ball unless a teammate steps in to set. After three minutes rotate. Substitutes rotate into specific game positions or after one full rotation.

MAXIM: *Allow the backcourt players to pass the majority of balls so the frontcourt players can concentrate on the attack.*

Team Serve Reception with Sheet—6's

Purpose: Serve reception training.

Team Goal: Five good passes to the setter in each rotation.

Description: Several sheets are sewn together and hung over the net so only the server's feet are visible under the sheet. On one side players are positioned for team serve reception and on the other side the rest of the players rotate serving responsibilities. The server calls out "ready" and serves primarily to backcourt receivers. Receiver passes to setter who sets the ball for the attack. Attackers approach and tip or jump set ball back to the servers. After five good passes rotate. Substitutes rotate into game positions or after one full rotation. It is important to stress good preparatory footwork. Players must be on their toes, ready to move quickly as the ball comes into view. There is less time to see where the ball is and react to it. Once the sheet is removed players appear to have a much longer time to see and prepare to pass the ball.

MAXIM: *Repeat drills until there is success.*

MAXIM: *Assume the served ball will come to you, and pass with confidence.*

Team Serve Reception, Attack—6's

Purpose: Transition: team serve reception, attack.

Goal:

1. Five good hits to rotate or
2. Three good hits in a row to rotate or
3. After good hit, back row player takes attacker's place, that is, back row becomes front row player. After ten good hits setter alters starting position.
4. Rotate on each good attack play. Count number of times it takes to rotate ball to original positions; strive to improve record.

Description: Team positioned for serve reception. Two or more servers alternate serving. Team pass, set, and attack utilizing play combinations. Add blockers.

MAXIM: *Blockers must learn attack patterns of opponents and the probabilities of each play, depending on the pass.*

MAXIM: *Setters must be sensitive to the pace of the game.*

Team Serve Reception, Attack, and Cover (Figure 7-31)

Purpose: Team serve reception, to attack training with emphasis on the cover.

Team Goal: Five good hits to rotate.

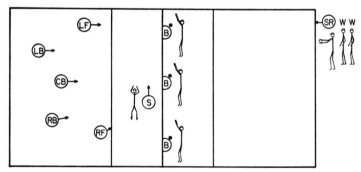

Figure 7-31

Description: Team in serve reception formation. One line of servers, one blocker opposite each attacker holding two volleyballs. First server serves ball and team receives, sets, attacks, and covers. Blockers do not block, but instead, if attack is in front of them they toss ball over the net to simulate a blocked ball. Team must recover ball, set, attack, and cover. Play continues until error is made. Substitute players into the rotation as desired. *Variation:* Place two blockers on a bench opposite each attacker. This presents a solid block, with a good cover being essential.

MAXIM: *Be ready to step in to set the bad pass. If you are not passing, your only responsibility is to be ready to assist in a difficult situation.*

MAXIM: *A good cover is like an offensive rebound in basketball. It gives your team a second chance to score.*

Team Transitions—6's vs. Server and Attacker Line (Figure 7-32)

Purpose: Transition: team serve reception to attack; team defense to attack.

Team Goal: Ten points then rotate. Rotate back to starting positions.

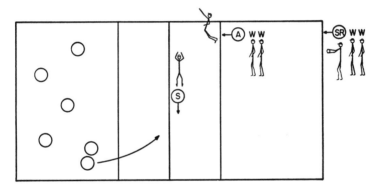

Figure 7-32

Description: Team vs. a line of attackers, servers, and one setter. Drill begins with a serve, team pass, set, attack, and cover. If attack is successful, ball is tossed to setter for attack from hitting line. Team defends against attack and plays out point. Coach tosses for several attacks and then instructs team to assume serve reception positions. If attack is unsuccessful off the serve reception, team continues receiving until a successful attack is made. Vary attack line position—right, center, and left. After ten points rotate. Two points are scored for a successful attack off serve reception; two points are scored for a successful attack off of a defensive play, and one point is scored for a ball passed over the net on a defensive play. Rotate after ten points. When team rotates back to original position groups change tasks.

MAXIM: Do not mistake activity for achievement. The coach must al-ways ask: What is the purpose of this drill? Is it game-related? Does it accomplish what I want? Is it helping us reach our goals?

Team Transitions—6's vs. Server and Multiple Attacker (Figure 7-33)

Purpose: Transition: serve reception to attack, team defense to attack, free ball to attack.

Goal: Specific time period.

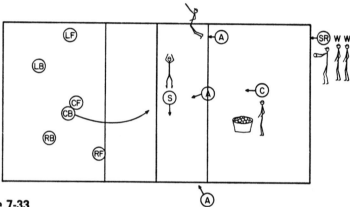

Figure 7-33

Description: A team of six vs. a group of servers, one setter, and three attackers. Server serves to team and they run system. Ball must be successfully played over the net to continue series, or serve is repeated. After successful attack, team moves quickly into defensive alignment. Coach tosses to setter who runs system. Team defends against attack and plays out point. Coach then tosses free ball to team and they play out point. Players rotate as coach indicates. Attackers on coach's side may block against team of six prior to their own attack.

MAXIM: Assign functions to individuals that they are capable of per-forming.

Team Transitions—6's vs. Server and Coach on Table (Figure 7-34)

Purpose: Transition: serve reception to attack, team defense to attack, free ball to attack.

Goal: Specific time period.

Description: A team of six on one side vs. a group of servers and coach on table. Team receives serves and runs system. Ball must be success-

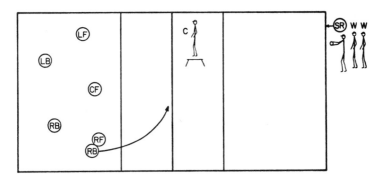

Figure 7-34

fully played over the net to continue series or serve is repeated. After successful attack, team moves quickly into defensive alignment, defends against coach attack, and plays out point. Coach may call "free ball" and toss ball over net for team to play out point. Coach hits or tosses about three times before next serve. Players rotate as coach indicates.

MAXIM: *Focus attention on the task, not on internal doubts or previous errors.*

MAXIM: *Drills must stress linking actions. There is a chain of responses, with and without the ball, that link individual and team movements until the ball is whistled dead.*

6 on 6 Team Free Ball Offense

Purpose: Transition: team free ball to attack.

Goal: Five to rotate.

Description: Two teams on court in starting defensive positions. Coach positioned off court tosses free ball to one side (offensive team). They pass, set, attack, and cover. Teams play out point, however the defensive team must return all balls with a pass, while the offensive team attacks. When rally ends, coach immediately tosses the next ball. After five good hits both teams rotate. When offensive team rotates back to original position, change tasks.

MAXIM: *Court talk (verbal communication) reduces errors, helps us adjust, helps us remember, helps us win. For example, "mine," "cover," "free ball," "no block," "in," "out."*

MAXIM: *To utilize the scrimmage tool most effectively stress scrimmage goals.*

MAXIM: *To utilize scrimmage time effectively do not shag ball at end of the rally. Have additional balls ready to serve immediately for the next play.*

MAXIM: *To make scrimmage more game-like, always use a referee (the coach, assistant coach, or substitute player).*

6 on 6 Scrimmage

Purpose: To stress the importance of winning consecutive points.

Goal: The first team to rotate back to its original position wins.

Description: One side serves the entire game. This is the defensive team. The other side is considered the offensive team. Points are scored on each rally by either the offensive or defensive team. The offensive team must score three consecutive points before rotating while the defensive team must score two consecutive points before rotating.

MAXIM: *Call time outs in scrimmages to give tactical instructions. Teach the response desired in the game situation.*

6 on 6 Scrimmage

Purpose: To stress the importance of winning consecutive points.

Goal: The first team to rotate back to its original position wins.

Description: Rotate only after server scores three points. Service changes sides as in a regulation game, however a team does not rotate and the same server continues to serve until three points are scored.

MAXIM: *Train attitude as well as skill. Determine the attitudes you want the team to have and stress them in practice.*

6 on 6 Scrimmage

Purpose: To give substitutes maximum practice in their specific game positions and to give the starting team the strongest competition possible.

Goal: The first team to 15 points wins.

Description: All substititues form one team and play their specific game positions, and do not rotate during the entire game. They play their strength and receive maximum practice for their role as substitute. The starting team rotates as in a regulation game.

MAXIM: *The most important condition for effectiveness is to utilize everyone's strongest points maximally.*

6 on 6 Scrimmage

Purpose: To stress concentration at the end of the game.

Goal: Win. Win by earning all five points consecutively (the perfect five).

Description: Game starts at ten points all. Play it out.

MAXIM: *When the game is close, do not take risks on serves.*

6 on 6 Scrimmage

Purpose: To stress concentration at the end of the game.

Goal: Win.

Description: The game score begins at 14–13.

MAXIM: *To play a better physical and mental game, expand your tactical horizons.*

6 on 6 Scrimmage

Purpose: Stress defense.

Goal: First to 15 wins.

Description: One team is the defensive team and it serves for the entire game. The defensive team scores one point for a successful block or a successful dig to the setter. The defensive team is not allowed to attack, but sends a free ball over to the offensive team. The offensive team scores one point for each rally won. The defensive team scores points for successful defensive plays while the offensive is rewarded for successful attacks.

MAXIM: *Make the best out of any situation that occurs in the game.*

6 on 6 Rotating Game (Figure 7-35)

Purpose: Transition, practice in each position.

Goal: Specific time period.

Description: Teams of six on each side. Receiving side has a permanent, nonrotating setter. Receiving team runs system off serve receiver. New

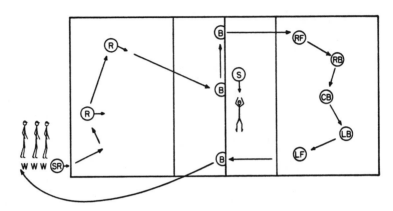

Figure 7-35

player rotates in after each serve as indicated in the diagram. All players rotate into all positions.

MAXIM: *Tip to the weakest backcourt player.*

MAXIM: *Understand and respect responsibilities of all court positions.*

MAXIM: *The main task of the coach is to train players through practice for the competitive game. This method is coaching through drills.*

Index